The Kallikak Family

DEBORAH KALLIKAK, AS SHE APPEARS TO-DAY AT THE TRAINING SCHOOL.

the Kallikak Family
A Study in the Heredity of Feeble-mindedness

BY

HENRY HERBERT GODDARD, PH.D.
Director of the Research Laboratory of the Training School at Vineland, New Jersey, for Feeble-minded Girls and Boys

MOONGLOW
2008

FIRST EDITION PUBLISHED BY
THE MACMILLAN COMPANY
SEPTEMBER, 1912

PRINT-ON-DEMAND REPRINT EDITION
BY WALTER LUKE III, MOONGLOW BOOKS
LICENSE: CREATIVE COMMONS
ATTRIBUTION-NONCOMMERCIAL-SHARE ALIKE 2.0

ISBN: 1440434506
EAN13: 978-1-4404-3450-1

TO
MR. SAMUEL S. FELS
FRIEND AND PHILANTHROPIST
A LAYMAN WITH THE SCIENTIST'S LOVE OF TRUTH
AND
THE TRUE CITIZEN'S LOVE OF HUMANITY
WHO MADE POSSIBLE THIS STUDY AND WHO HAS
FOLLOWED THE WORK FROM ITS INCIPIENCY
WITH KINDLY CRITICISM AND ADVICE
THIS BOOK
IS DEDICATED

Preface

On September 15, 1906, the Training School for Backward and Feeble-minded Children at Vineland, New Jersey, opened a laboratory and a Department of Research for the study of feeble-mindedness.

A beginning was made in studying the mental condition of the children who lived in the Institution, with a view to determining the mental and physical peculiarities of the different grades and types, to getting an accurate record of what deficiencies each child had and what he was capable of doing, with the hope that in time these records could be correlated with the condition of the nervous system of the child, if he should die while in the Institution and an autopsy should be allowed.

As soon as possible after the beginning of this work, a definite start was made toward determining the cause of feeble-mindedness. After some preliminary work, it was concluded that the only way to get the information needed was by sending trained workers to the homes of the children, to learn by careful and wise questioning the facts that could be obtained. It was a great surprise to us to discover so much mental defect in the families of so many of these children. The results of the study of more than 300 families will soon be published, showing that about 65 per cent of these children have the hereditary taint.

PREFACE

The present study of the Kallikak family is a genuine story of real people. The name is, of course, fictitious, as are all of the names throughout the story. The results here presented come after two years of constant work, investigating the conditions of this family.

Some readers may question how it has been possible to get such definite data in regard to people who lived so long ago.

A word of explanation is hence in order. In the first place, the family itself proved to be a notorious one, so the people, in the community where the present generations are living, know of them; they knew their parents and grandparents; and the older members knew them farther back, because of the reputation they had always borne. Secondly, the reputation which the Training School has in the State is such that all have been willing to cooperate as soon as they understood the purpose and plan of the work. This has been of great help. Thirdly, the time devoted to this investigation must not be overlooked. A hasty investigation could never have produced the results which we have reached. Oftentimes a second, a third, a fifth, or a sixth visit has been necessary in order to develop an acquaintance and relationship with these families which induced them gradually to relate things which they otherwise had not recalled or did not care to tell. Many an important item has been gathered after several visits to these homes. Chapter IV will throw still more light on the method used.

If the reader is inclined to the view that we must have called a great many people feeble-minded who were not so, let him be assured that this is not the case. On the contrary, we have preferred to err on the other side, and we have not marked people feeble-minded unless the case was such that we could substantiate it beyond a reasonable doubt. If there was good reason to call them normal, we have so marked them. If not, and we are unable to decide in our own minds, we have generally left them unmarked. In a few cases, we have marked them normal or feeble-minded, with a question mark. By this is meant that we have studied the case and alter deliberation are still in doubt, but the probabilities are "N" or "F" as indicated. The mere fact of the doubt shows, however, that they are at least border-line cases.

To the scientific reader we would say that the data here presented are, we believe, accurate to a high degree. It is true that we have made rather dogmatic statements and have drawn conclusions that do not seem scientifically warranted from the data. We have done this because it seems necessary to make these statements and conclusions for the benefit of the lay reader, and it was impossible to present in this book all of the data that would substantiate them. We have, as a matter of fact, drawn upon the material which is soon to be presented in a larger book. The reference to Mendelism is an illustration of what we mean. It is, as it is given here, meager and inadequate, and the assumption that the given law applies to human heredity is an assumption so far as the data presented are concerned. We would ask that the scientist reserve judgment and wait for the larger book for the proof of these statements and for an adequate discussion of Mendelism in relation to the problem.

The necessary expense for this study, as well as for all of the work of the Research Laboratory, has been met by voluntary contributions from philanthropic men and women, who believe that here is an opportunity to benefit humanity, such as is hardly equaled elsewhere.

We take this means of expressing to them our deep appreciation of their sympathy and generosity. I wish also to make special mention of the indefatigable industry, wisdom, tact, and judgment of our field workers who have gathered these facts and whose results, although continually checked up, have stood every test put upon them as to their accuracy and value.

PREFACE

The work on this particular family has been done by Elizabeth S. Kite, to whom I am also indebted for practically all of Chapter IV.

I am also greatly indebted to my assistants in the laboratory, for help in preparing the charts, keeping the records, and correcting manuscript and proof.

To Superintendent Edward R. Johnstone, whose wisdom and foresight led to the establishment of this Department of Research, whose help, sympathy, and encouragement have been constant throughout the work of preparing this study, the thanks and gratitude of the entire group of readers who find in these facts any help toward the solution of the problems that they are facing, are due.

Henry H. Goddard.

Vineland, N.J.,
September, 1912.

Contents

		PAGE
Preface	. . . .	*viii*
I. The Story of Deborah	. . . .	17
II. The Data	. . . . . .	30
The Charts	. . . . .	47
III. What it Means	. . . . .	64
IV. Further Facts About the Kallikak Family	.	78
V. What is to be Done?	. . . .	102

List of Illustrations

Deborah Kallikak as she appears To-day at the Training School . . . . *Frontispiece*

	PAGE
Deborah at the Sewing Machine . . .	20
Deborah as Waitress	20
Specimens of Deborah's Handiwork . . .	23
Deborah, aged Fifteen.	26
Deborah, aged Seventeen	26
Last Home of Millard Kallikak	36
Esther, Daughter of "Daddy" Kallikak . . .	36
Ruins of Mountain Hut built by Martin Kallikak Jr.	39
Site of Mountain Home of Millard Kallikak . .	39
Great-grandson of "Daddy" Kallikak . . .	88
Melinda, Daughter of "Jemima"	88
Great-grandchildren of "Old Sal" . . .	91
Children of Guss Saunders, with their Grandmother	91

Chapter I

The Story of Deborah

One bright October day, fourteen years ago, there came to the Training School at Vineland, a little eight-year-old girl. She had been born in an almshouse. Her mother had afterwards married, not the father of this child, but the prospective father of another child, and later had divorced him and married another man, who was also the father of some of her children. She had been led to do this through the efforts of well-meaning people who felt that it was a great misfortune for a child to be born into the world illegitimately. From their standpoint the argument was good, because the mother with four or five younger children was unable to provide adequately for this little girl, whom both husbands refused to support.

On the plea that the child did not get along well at school and might possibly be feeble-minded, she gained admission to the Training School, there to begin a career which has been interesting and valuable to the Institution, and which has led to an investigation that cannot fail to prove of great social import.

The following are extracts from her history since she came to the Institution: —

From Admission Blanks,
    Nov. '97. — Average size and weight. No peculiarity in form or size of head. Staring expression. Jerking movement

in walking. No bodily deformity. Mouth shut. Washes and dresses herself, except fastening clothes. Understands commands. Not very obedient. Knows a few letters. Cannot read nor count. Knows all the colors. Not fond of music. Power of memory poor. Listens well. Looks steadily. Good imitator. Can use a needle. Can carry wood and fill a kettle. Can throw a ball, but cannot catch. Sees and hears well. Right-handed. Excitable but not nervous. Not affectionate and quite noisy. Careless in dress. Active. Obstinate and destructive. Does not mind slapping and scolding. Grandmother somewhat deficient. Grandfather periodical drunkard and mentally deficient. Been to school. No results.

From Institution Reports: —

Jan. '99. — Conduct better. Counts 1-10 and 10-1. Knows at sight and can write from memory "see," "me," "ran," "man," "rat," "can." Weaves difficult mat in steps of 1 and 3, but requires much assistance.

Feb. '99.— Counts 1-30; writes 1—15. Orderly. Folds neatly.

March, '99. — Draws circle and square. Writes 1-29. Combines simple numbers.

April, '99. — Conduct quite bad — impudent and growing worse. Transferred from Seguin Cottage to Wilbur for a while. Seems some better.

SCHOOL. *Dec.* '00. Disobedient. Graceful. Good in drill. Can copy. Knows a number of words. Writes them from memory. Reads a little. Adds with objects. Counts and knows value of numbers. Does all ladder and pole drills nicely. Good in entertainment work. Memorizes quickly. Can always be relied upon for either speaking or singing. Marches well. A good captain. Knows "Halt," "Right," and "Left Face" and "Forward March." Always in step.

MUSIC. Knows different notes. Plays "Jesus, Lover of my Soul" nicely. Plays scale of C and F on cornet.

May, '01. — Plays scales of C and F and first two exercises in "Beginners' Band Book" on cornet. She plays by ear. She has not learned to read the notes of these two scales, simply because she will not put her mind to it. She has played hymns in simple time, but the fingering has had to be written for her.

SCHOOL. Excellent worker in gardening class. Has just completed a very good diagram of our garden to show at Annual Meeting.

COTTAGE. Helps make beds and waits on table, is quick with her work, but is very noisy.

Oct. '01. — Has nearly finished outlining a pillow sham. Can do very good work when she tries.

ENGLISH. Does better in number work than in any other branch. Her mind wanders a great deal. In the midst of a lesson, that she has apparently paid a great deal of attention to, she will ask a question that has no bearing on the lesson at all. Is slow to learn.

Nov. '01. — Is very good in number work, especially in addition. Can add 25 and 15. Spells a few words, such as "wind," "blows," "flowers." Writes fairly well from copy if she tries. Her attention is very hard to keep. Is restless in class. Likes to be first in everything. The one thing she does best in school is to add numbers with pegs. Knows about fifteen words, such as "cat," "fan," "run," "man." She could learn more in school if she would pay attention, but her mind seems away off from the subject in discussion. Could play scale of C and F on cornet and would play some by

Deborah at the Sewing Machine

Deborah as Waitress

ear if she could have kept up her lessons. Was taken out on account of sore throat.

Nov. '04.— Understands how to make bead chains. Has made four. Knows how to use a sewing machine. Has made a shirtwaist. Uses tape measure accurately. Can play on cornet four hard band pieces and three solos, also reads at sight easy songs and hymns. Band pieces are: "Attention, March!" "Quick Step Sterling," "Onward, Christian Soldiers," and "Star-spangled Banner." Solos are: "America," "Old Black Joe," and "Onward, Christian Soldiers." Conduct at school, fair.

Jan. '07.—Took the part of Mrs. Doe in "Fun in a Photograph Gallery."

Feb. '08. — Can write a fairly good story, but spells very few words. Has little idea of the use of capitals, It is difficult for her to separate her sentences. Drawing, painting, coloring, and any kind of hand work she does quite nicely. In clay modeling, her idea of form is quite good. Is much improved in conduct. Does not act so wild in class.

In wood-carving class, she starts a thing she wants to do very enthusiastically, but if it takes her very long, her interest flags and she has to be spurred on by the thought of the result when well done. This year she has made a carved book rest with mission ends and is now working on a shirtwaist box with mortise and tenon joints and lap joints. The top will be paneled. She can do most of her own marking when shown how.

Has made a great improvement in "Band" during the last year. Can get a better tone on the cornet and more volume. Reads by note all music that she plays. Plays second cornet parts to about twenty-five pieces.

Jan. '09. — Has embroidered the front of a shirtwaist and the front gore of a skirt. She has shown a great amount of patience, perseverance, and judgment in her work this year, has been anxious to do her work, and has been a good girl. In wood carving she is doing much more careful work than last year.

Has made a large "Skolcroft" chair with only a little help in putting it into clamps. Did her own measuring and carved the wood. She filled the wood herself before staining. This she had never done before.

June, '09. — Made the suit which she had embroidered earlier in the year, using the machine in making it. Helped F. B. put her chair together and really acted as a teacher in showing her how to upholster it. Will be a helper in wood-carving class this summer.

Took important part in the Christmas play of 1908 and was a "Fan Girl" in the Japanese play given Annual Day, 1909.

Mar. '11.—Works just about the same in wood-carving class as she has other years. Can work very rapidly when she tries, but does not very often try. Does not have much confidence in herself when marking out her work, but when urged, keeps trying until she gets it right. Is making a large dressing case this year. Is doing very nice work, especially in physical culture class.

May, '11. — Finished her dressing case, but was careless towards the last, so it is not quite as nice as was expected. Made a very handsome embroidered linen dress (satin stitch and eyelets), also an embroidered corset cover. Made up both pieces under direction. Can write a well-worded story, but has to have more than half the words spelled for her. Knows very few of her number combinations. Retains a great many interesting facts connected with nature work.

The reader will see that Deborah's teachers have worked with her faithfully and carefully, hoping for progress, even

SPECIMENS OF DEBORAH'S HANDIWORK.

seeing it where at a later date it became evident that no real advance had been made. Note the oft-repeated "She could if she would," or "If she would only pay attention," and similar expressions, which show the unwillingness of the teachers to admit even to themselves that she is really feeble-minded. In the earlier records it was noted that Deborah was not fond of music, while in later reports it is shown to be her one great accomplishment. To-day she is a woman of twenty-two. The consensus of opinion of those who have known her for the last fourteen years in the Institution is as follows: —

> "She is cheerful, inclined to be quarrelsome, very active and restless, very affectionate, willing, and tries; is quick and excitable, fairly good-tempered. Learns a new occupation quickly, but requires a half hour or twenty-four repetitions to learn four lines. Retains well what she has once learned. Needs close supervision. Is bold towards strangers, kind towards animals. Can run an electric sewing machine, cook, and do practically everything about the house. Has no noticeable defect. She is quick and observing, has a good memory, writes fairly, does excellent work in wood-carving and kindergarten, is excellent in imitation. Is a poor reader, and poor at numbers. Does fine basketry and gardening. Spelling is poor; music is excellent; sewing excellent; excellent in entertainment work. Very fond of children and good in helping care for them. Has a good sense of order and cleanliness. Is sometimes very stubborn and obstinate. Is not always truthful and has been known to steal, although does not have a reputation for this. Is proud of her clothes. Likes pretty dresses and likes to help in other cottages, even to temporarily taking charge of a group."

The children at the Training School write letters to Santa Claus asking for such things as they want for Christmas. Here are Deborah's requests each year, beginning with '99, when she was ten years old: —

'99. — Book and harmonica.
'00. — Book, comb, paints, and doll.
'01. — Book, mittens, toy piano, handkerchief, slate pencil.
'02. — Wax doll, ribbon, music box.
'03. — Post cards, colored ribbons, gloves and shears.
'04. — Trunk, music box, Fairy Tales, games, ribbons, big doll.
'05. — Ribbons of different colors, games, handkerchiefs, music box, Fairy Tales.
'06. — Pair of stockings, ribbons, rubbers.
'07. — Watch, red ribbon, brush and comb, paper.
'08. — Three yards of lawn, rubbers.
'09. — Nice shoes, pink, dark blue, and white ribbons.
'10. — Money for dentist bill.
'11. — Rubbers, three shirts, blue scarf, three yards linen, two yards lawn for fancy work.

It will be remembered that in her history, number was mentioned as being one of her strong points. Indeed, she had a great deal of thorough drill in this branch. In a recent testing to determine how much of this she still retained, or whether the work had been of any value as mental discipline, the results were negative. It was discovered that she could neither add nor subtract, except where it was a question of concrete objects connected with her daily life. For example, she can set a table and wait on it very nicely. She can put the right number of plates at the head of the table, if she knows the people who are

AGE 17.

AGE 15.

DEBORAH.

to sit there, but at a table with precisely the same number of strangers, she fails in making the correct count.

At a recent test made before a prominent scientist, the question was asked, "How many are 12 less 3?" She thought for a moment, looked around the room and finally answered, "Nine." "Correct," said her questioner. "Do you know how I did it?" she asked, delighted at her success. "I counted on my fingers."

Some of the questions asked her and her answers are as follows: —

Q. There are ten people to eat dinner. Seven have eaten. For how many must you keep dinner warm?
A. Three.
Q. Suppose you had eight ergographs and sell six. How many would be left?
A. (after twenty-eight seconds' pondering). Two.
Q. Suppose you had eight Deltas and gave two away. What would you have left?
A. Five.
Q. Suppose there are eight at the table and two leave. How many would remain?
A. (after thirteen seconds). Six.

By the Binet Scale this girl showed, in April, 1910, the mentality of a nine-year-old child with two points over; January, 1911, 9 years, 1 point; September, 1911, 9 years, 2 points; October, 1911, 9 years, 3 points. She answers correctly all of the questions up to age 7 except the repetition of five figures, where she transposes two of them. She does not read the selection in the required time, nor does she remember what she reads. In counting the stamps, her first answer was "ten cents," which she later corrected. Under age 9, none of her definitions are "better than by use" — "Fork is to eat with," "Chair to sit on," etc. She can sometimes arrange the weights in their proper order and at other times not. The same is true of putting the three words into a sentence. She does not know money. Her definitions of abstract terms are very poor, in some cases barely passable, nor can she put together the dissected sentences. She rhymes "storm" with "spring," and "milk" with "mill," afterwards using "bill," "will," "till."

In the revised questions, she does not draw the design which is Question 2 in age 10, nor does she resist suggestion, Question 4 in age 12. To the first part of Question 5, age 12, she answered, "A bird hanging from the limb," and to the second part, "Some one was very sick."

This is a typical illustration of the mentality of a high-grade feeble-minded person, the moron, the delinquent, the kind of girl or woman that fills our reformatories. They are wayward, they get into all sorts of trouble and difficulties, sexually and otherwise, and yet we have been accustomed to account for their defects on the basis of viciousness, environment, or ignorance.

It is also the history of the same type of girl in the public school. Rather good-looking, bright in appearance, with many attractive ways, the teacher clings to the hope, indeed insists, that such a girl will come out all right. Our work with Deborah convinces us that such hopes are delusions.

Here is a child who has been most carefully guarded. She has been persistently trained since she was eight years old, and yet nothing has been accomplished in the direction of higher intelligence or general education. To-day if this young woman were to leave the Institution, she would at once become a prey to the designs of evil men or evil women and would lead a life that would be vicious, immoral, and criminal, though because of her mentality she herself would not be responsible. There is nothing that she might not be led into, because she has no power of control, and all her instincts and appetites are in the direction that would lead to vice.

We may now repeat the ever insistent question, and this time we indeed have good hope of answering it. The question is, "How do we account for this kind of individual?" The answer is in a word "Heredity," — bad stock. We must recognize that the human family shows varying stocks or strains that are as marked and that breed as true as anything in plant or animal life.

Formerly such a statement would have been a guess, an hypothesis. We submit in the following pages what seems to us conclusive evidence of its truth.

Chapter II

The Data

The Vineland Training School has for two years employed field workers. These are women highly trained, of broad human experience, and interested in social problems. As a result of weeks of residence at the Training School, they become acquainted with the condition of the feeble-minded. They study all the grades, note their peculiarities, and acquaint themselves with the methods of testing and recognizing them. They then go out with an introduction from the Superintendent to the homes of the children and there ask that all the facts which are available may be furnished, in order that we can know more about the child and be better able to care for him and more wisely train him.

Sometimes all necessary information is obtained from the one central source, but more often, especially where the parents are themselves defective, many visits to other homes must be made. Parents often send the field worker to visit near and distant relatives as well as neighbors, employers, teachers, physicians, ministers, overseers of the poor, almshouse directors, etc. These must be interviewed and all the information thus obtained must be weighed and much of it verified by repeated visits to the same locality before an accurate chart of the particular child's heredity can be made.

In determining the mental condition of people in the earlier generations (that is, as to whether they were feeble-minded or not), one proceeds in the same way as one does to determine the character of a Washington or a Lincoln or any other man of the past. Recourse is had to original documents whenever possible. In the case of defectives, of course, there are not many original documents. Oftentimes the absence of these, where they are to be expected, is of itself significant. For instance, the absence of a record of marriage is often quite as significant as its presence. Some record or memory is generally obtainable of how the person lived, how he conducted himself, whether he was able to make a living, how he brought up his children, what was his reputation in the community; these facts are frequently sufficient to enable one to determine, with a high degree of accuracy, whether the individual was normal or otherwise. Sometimes the condition is marked by the presence of other factors. For example, if a man was strongly alcoholic, it is almost impossible to determine whether he was also feeble-minded, because the reports usually declare that the only trouble with him was that he was always drunk, and they say if he had been sober, he would have been all right. This may be true, but on the other hand, it is quite possible that he was feeble-minded also.

After some experience, the field worker becomes expert in inferring the condition of those persons who are not seen, from the similarity of the language used in describing them to that used in describing persons whom she has seen.

In Deborah's case, the woman first visited was the one who interested herself in the child and its mother when the latter had just given birth to her baby in the almshouse. From this woman was learned the subsequent history of Deborah's mother as given in the first part of this description. But references, supplied by her, soon led to further discoveries. The present family was found living within twenty miles of what was afterwards learned to be its ancestral home and in a region that was neither the slums of a city nor the wild desolation of the extreme rural community, but rather in the midst of a populous farming country, one of the best districts in the State. Thorough and carefully conducted investigations in the small town and among the farmers of this region showed that the family had always been notorious for the number of defectives and delinquents it had produced; and this notoriety made it possible to trace them back for no less than six generations.

It was determined to make a survey of the entire family and to discover the condition, as far as possible, of every person in each generation.

The surprise and horror of it all was that no matter where we traced them, whether in the prosperous rural district, in the city slums to which some had drifted, or in the more remote mountain regions, or whether it was a question of the second or the sixth generation, an appalling amount of defectiveness was everywhere found.

In the course of the work of tracing various members of the family, our field worker occasionally found herself in the midst of a good family of the same name, which apparently was in no way related to the girl whose ancestry we were investigating. In such cases, there was nothing to be done but to beat a retreat and start again in another direction. However, these cases became so frequent that there gradually grew the conviction that ours must be a degenerate offshoot from an older family of better stock. Definite work was undertaken in order to locate the point at which the separation took place. Over and over, the investigation was laid aside in sheer despair of ever being able to find absolute proofs or to establish missing links in the testimony. Then some freshly discovered facts, that came often quite unexpectedly, would throw new light on the situation, and the work would be resumed.

The great-great-grandfather of Deborah[1] was Martin Kallikak.[1] That we knew. We had also traced the good family, before alluded to, back to an ancestor belonging to an older generation than this Martin Kallikak, but bearing the same name. He was the father of a large family. His eldest son was named Frederick, but there was no son by the name of Martin. Consequently, no connection could be made. Many months later, a granddaughter of Martin revealed in a burst of confidence the situation. She told us (and this was afterwards fully verified) that Martin had a half brother Frederick, — and that Martin never had an own brother "because," as she now naively expressed it, "you see, his mother had him before she was married." Deeper scrutiny into the life of Martin Kallikak Sr., which was made possible through well-preserved family records, enabled us to complete the story.

When Martin Sr., of the good family, was a boy of fifteen, his father died, leaving him without parental care or oversight. Just before attaining his majority, the young man joined one of the numerous military companies that were formed to protect the country at the beginning of the Revolution. At one of the taverns frequented by the militia he met a feeble-minded girl by whom he became the father of a feeble-minded son. This child was given, by its mother, the name of the father in full, and thus has been handed down to posterity the father's name and the mother's mental capacity. This illegitimate boy was Martin Kallikak Jr., the great-great-grandfather of our Deborah, and from him have come four hundred and eighty descendants. One hundred and forty-three of these, we have conclusive proof, were or are feeble-minded, while only forty-six have been found normal. The rest are unknown or doubtful.

Among these four hundred and eighty descendants, thirty-six have been illegitimate.

1 All names, both Christian and sur-names, are fictitious..

There have been thirty-three sexually immoral persons, mostly prostitutes.

There have been twenty-four confirmed alcoholics.

There have been three epileptics.

Eighty-two died in infancy.

Three were criminal.

Eight kept houses of ill fame.

These people have married into other families, generally of about the same type, so that we now have on record and charted eleven hundred and forty-six individuals.

Of this large group, we have discovered that two hundred and sixty-two were feeble-minded, while one hundred and ninety-seven are considered normal, the remaining five hundred and eighty-one being still undetermined. ("Undetermined," as here employed, often means not that we knew nothing about the person, but that we could not decide. They are people we can scarcely recognize as normal; frequently they are not what we could call good members of society. But it is very difficult to decide without more facts whether the condition that we find or that we learn about, as in the case of older generations, is or was really one of feeble-mindedness.)

In 1803, Martin Kallikak Jr., otherwise known as the "Old Horror," married Rhoda Zabeth, a normal woman. (See Chart II.) They had ten children, of whom one died in infancy and another died at birth with the mother. Of those who lived, the oldest was Millard, the direct ancestor of our Deborah. He married Althea Haight, and they had fifteen children, of whom more later.

The next born of Martin Jr. was Nathan, known in the community as "Daddy" (see Chart III),[1] who died at the advanced age of ninety-three. He was the father of six children. One of his sons was a criminal, a horse thief, who also stole a flock of

[1] It is important to trace out in detail these relationships on the charts.

sheep which the owner all unwittingly helped him to drive away. Three other children of "Daddy" married and themselves had children. These are all families about whose mentality it is difficult to decide. They are all peculiar, but more respectable than some other branches of this family. One is dead. The sixth, a daughter, is feeble-minded and sexually immoral. She married a man who was feeble-minded and alcoholic. Of her six children, two at least are feeble-minded. Whether her husband is the father of all of the children is very doubtful. Sexual immorality and alcoholism are prevalent in this family. One of the sons married a feeble-minded woman who came from feeble-minded stock. They had six children, all of whom were feeble-minded. One of these is of the Mongolian type, an interesting fact, as it shows that this particular form of arrest of development may occur in a defective family.

Martin Jr.'s third child was James (Chart II), who went away, and we know nothing about him.

Martin Jr.'s fourth child, "Old Sal" (Chart IV), was feeble-minded and she married a feeble-minded man. Two of their children are undetermined, but one of these had at least one feeble-minded grandchild; the other, an alcoholic man, had three feeble-minded grandchildren, one of whom is in the Training School at Vineland. She is thus a cousin of Deborah — a fact not known until this study was made. The two other children of Old Sal were feeble-minded, married feeble-minded wives, and had large families of defective children and grandchildren, as will be seen in the chart.

The fifth child of Martin Jr. was Jemima (Chart V), feeble-minded and sexually immoral. She lived with a feeble-minded man named Horser, to whom she was supposed to have been married. Of her five children, three are known to have been feeble-minded, two are undetermined. From these again, have come a large number of feeble-minded children

LAST HOME OF MILLARD KALLIKAK

ESTHER, DAUGHTER OF "DADDY" KALLIKAK

and grandchildren. Jemima had an illegitimate son by a man who was high in the Nation's offices. This son married a feeble-minded girl and they had feeble-minded children, and grandchildren.

The sixth child of Martin Jr., known as "Old Moll" (Chart VI), was feeble-minded, alcoholic, epileptic, and sexually immoral. She had three illegitimate children who were sent to the almshouse, and from there bound out to neighboring farmers. One of these turned out normal, one was feeble-minded, and the other undetermined. Neither of the two older ones had any children. The third child, a daughter, was tubercular, but nothing is known of her descendants, except that there were several children and grandchildren.

The seventh child of Martin Jr. was a daughter, Sylvia (Chart VII), who seemed to be a normal woman. She was taken very young by a good family who brought her up carefully. She later married a normal man. Although we have marked her normal, she was always peculiar. All her children and grandchildren were either normal or are undetermined.

The youngest child of Martin Jr. who lived to grow up was Amy Jones, also normal. (Chart VIII.) She, too, was taken into a good family and married a normal man, and lived to be very old. Two of Amy's children died in infancy. Of two others, one was normal and one feeble-minded. This latter married a normal man and had one feeble-minded and immoral daughter; five other children are undetermined.

We now return to Martin Jr.'s oldest son, Millard (Chart IX), to take up the story of his descendants, of whom our girl Deborah is one.

Millard married Althea Haight about 1830. They had fifteen children born in the following years: 1830, 1831, 1832, 1834, 1836, 1838, 1840, 1841, 1843, 1845, 1847, 1849, 1851, 1854, 1856. The mother died in 1857. This mother, Althea Haight, was feeble-minded. That she came from a feeble-minded family is evidenced by the fact that she had at least one feeble-minded brother, while of her mother it was said that the "devil himself could not live with her." The feeble-minded brother had six children, of whom three are known to have been feeble-minded. He had seven grandchildren who were feeble-minded, and no less than nine feeble-minded great-grandchildren. (These are not shown on the chart.)

The oldest child of Millard and Althea was a daughter who grew up a feeble-minded and immoral woman. She had several husbands, but only one of her children lived to be old enough to marry. This one, a daughter of illegitimate birth, married a man of good family who was a confirmed alcoholic. Their children are all undetermined, except one who was normal.

The second child of Millard, a daughter, was a bad character. We know of one illegitimate and feeble-minded son who married a feeble-minded and immoral girl. They had four children, but all died in infancy. This wife was also the mother of an illegitimate son, who was feeble-minded and sexually immoral.

The third child of Millard was Justin (Chart IX, section E), the grandfather of our Deborah. His family we shall discuss later.

According to Mendelian expectation, all of the children of Millard Kallikak and Althea Haight should have been feeble-minded, because the parents were such. The facts, so far as known, confirm this expectation, with the exception of the fourth child, a daughter, who was taken into a good family and grew up apparently a normal woman. She married a normal man and they had one son who was normal. He married a normal woman and they have two children, a boy and girl, who are normal and above average intelligence.

The fifth child was Albert, feeble-minded, who died at twenty-five, unmarried.

Ruins of Mountain Hut Built by Martin Kallikak Jr. 1805.

Site of Mountain Home of Millard Kallikak, where Fifteen of His Children were Born.

The sixth child was Warren, who had four children, three of whom were feeble-minded and of very doubtful morality. Each of the three had feeble-minded children. One of these, Guss by name, was specially loose and much mixed in his marital relations.

The seventh child was Lavinia, who died unmarried at the age of thirty-nine. She had been brought up in a good family and never manifested any of those characteristics that indicate feeble-mindedness.

The eighth was Cordelia, who died at nine; condition unknown.

The ninth was Prince, who died at four years.

The tenth was Paula, feeble-minded; married and had four children. Her husband and children are undetermined.

Then comes Gregory, the eleventh, who was feeble-minded and alcoholic. He married an alcoholic and syphilitic woman, mentality difficult to determine. They had seven children, of whom two were feeble-minded, syphilitic, alcoholic, and sexually immoral. One died of delirium tremens, the other of alcoholism, leaving a long line of descendants. The other children died young, except one daughter who has a feeble-minded grandchild who cannot speak.

The twelfth child was Harriet, feeble-minded, twice married, but without children.

The thirteenth, Sanders, who was drowned as a young man, was feeble-minded and sexually immoral.

The fourteenth was Thomas, feeble-minded, alcoholic, and sexually immoral. He died from over self-indulgence. He was married and had a daughter, but her condition as well as her mother's is unknown.

The last child was Joseph, feeble-minded. He married his first cousin, Eva Haight, who was also feeble-minded. They had five children, two dying in infancy, and the rest feeble-minded.

Of their nineteen grandchildren, five died in infancy, one is undetermined, and the remaining thirteen are all feeble-minded.

Millard Kallikak married for his second wife a normal woman, a sister of a man of prominence. She was, however, of marked peculiarity. By her, he had three children; two died in infancy. The one who grew to manhood was alcoholic and syphilitic. He ran off with the wife of his nephew, who was about his own age. His mental condition is undetermined. He was killed by an accident a few years later.

We now return to the third born of this family, Justin Kallikak, the grandfather of our Deborah (Chart IX, section E). He was feeble-minded, alcoholic, and sexually immoral. He married Eunice Barrah, who belonged to a family of dull mentality. Her mother and paternal grandfather were feeble-minded, and the grandfather had a brother that was feeble-minded. That brother had at least six descendants who were feeble-minded. The father, also, had a brother feeble-minded who had eleven children, grandchildren, and great-grandchildren who were feeble-minded. (Not shown).

The children of Deborah's grandparents, Justin and Eunice, were as follows: first, Martha, the mother of our Deborah, whose story has already been partly told. This woman is supposed to have had three illegitimate children before Deborah was born. They died in infancy. The next younger half sister of Deborah was placed out by a charitable organization when very young. From their records we learn that in five years she had been tried in thirteen different families and by all found impossible. In one of these she set the barn on fire. When found by our field worker, she had grown to be a girl of twenty, pretty, graceful, but of low mentality. She had already followed the instinct implanted in her by her mother, and was on the point of giving birth to an illegitimate child. She was sent to a hospital. The child died, and then the girl was placed permanently in a home for feeble-minded. An own brother of this girl was placed out in a private family. When a little under sixteen, his foster mother died and her husband married again. Thus the boy was turned adrift. Having been well trained, and being naturally of an agreeable disposition, he easily found employment. Bad company, however, soon led to his discharge. He has now drifted into one of our big cities. It requires no prophet to predict his future.

The last family of half brothers and sisters of Deborah are, at present, living with the mother and her second husband. The oldest three of these are distinctly feeble-minded. Between them and the two younger children there was a stillbirth and a miscarriage. The little ones appear normal and test normal for their ages, but there is good reason to believe that they will develop the same defect as they grow older.

Besides the mother of Deborah, Justin and Eunice had ten other children, of whom six died in infancy. One of the daughters, Margaret, was taken by a good family when a very small child. When she was about thirteen, she visited her parents for a few weeks. While her mother was away at work, her father, who was a drunken brute, committed incest with her. When the fact became known in her adopted home, she was placed in the almshouse. The child born there soon died, and she was again received into the family where she formerly lived. The care with which she was surrounded prevented her from becoming a vicious woman. Although of dull mentality, she was a good and cheerful worker. When about thirty-five, she married a respectable workingman but has had no children by him.

Another daughter, Abigail, feeble-minded, married a feeble-minded man by whom she had two feeble-minded children, besides a third that died in infancy. She later married a normal man.

The next child of Justin and Eunice was Beede, who is feeble-minded. He married a girl who left him before their child was born. He lives at present with a very low, immoral woman.

The youngest child of Justin and Eunice was a son, Gaston, feeble-minded and a horse thief; he removed to a distant town where he married. He has one child; mentality of both mother and child undetermined.

This is the ghastly story of the descendants of Martin Kallikak Sr., from the nameless feeble-minded girl.

Although Martin himself paid no further attention to the girl nor her child, society has had to pay the heavy price of all the evil he engendered.

Martin Sr., on leaving the Revolutionary Army, straightened up and married a respectable girl of good family, and through that union has come another line of descendants of radically different character. These now number four hundred and ninety-six in direct descent. All of them are normal people. Three men only have been found among them who were somewhat degenerate, but they were not defective. Two of these were alcoholic, and the other sexually loose.

All of the legitimate children of Martin Sr. Married into the best families in their state, the descendants of colonial governors, signers of the Declaration of Independence, soldiers and even the founders of a great university. Indeed, in this family and its collateral branches, we find nothing but good representative citizenship. There are doctors, lawyers, judges, educators, traders, landholders, in short, respectable citizens, men and women prominent in every phase of social life. They have scattered over the United States and are prominent in their communities wherever they have gone. Half a dozen towns in New Jersey are named from the families into which Martin's descendants have married. There have been no feeble-minded among them; no illegitimate children; no immoral women; only one man was sexually loose. There has been no epilepsy, no criminals, no keepers of houses of prostitution. Only fifteen children have died in infancy. There has been one "insane," a case of religious mania, perhaps inherited, but not from the Kallikak side. The appetite for strong drink has been present here and there in this family from the beginning. It was in Martin Sr., and was cultivated at a time when such practices were common everywhere. But while the other branch of the family has had twenty-four victims of habitual drunkenness, this side scores only two.

The charts of these two families follow.

The Charts

The Charts

Chart I shows the line of descent of the Kallikak family from their first colonial ancestor. It was Martin who divided it into a bad branch on one hand and a good branch on the other. Each of these branches is traced through the line of the eldest son down to a person of the present generation. On the bad side it ends with Deborah Kallikak, an inmate of the Training School at Vineland, on the good side with the son of a prominent and wealthy citizen of the same family name, now resident of another State.

Chart II shows the children of Martin Sr. by his wife and by the nameless feeble-minded girl, and also the children of Martin Jr.

Then follow Charts III to IX and A to K, giving in detail each of these two branches, the upper series being the normal family, the descendants of Martin Kallikak Sr. through his wife: the lower is the bad family, his descendants through the nameless feeble-minded girl who was not his wife.

Explanation of Symbols

Individuals are represented by squares and circles, the squares being males, the circles, females. Black squares and circles (with a white "F") mean feeble-minded individuals; N means normal persons.

The clear squares or circles indicate that the mentality of the person is undetermined.

"d. inf." means died in infancy.

A horizontal or slightly oblique line connects persons who are mated. Unless otherwise indicated, they are supposed to have been legally married.

The symbols dependent from the same horizontal line are for brothers and sisters.

A vertical line connecting this horizontal line with an individual or with a line connecting two individuals, indicates the parent or parents of the fraternity.

Letters placed around the symbol for an individual are as follows: A — Alcoholic, meaning decidedly intemperate, a drunkard; B — Blind; C — Criminalistic; D — Deaf; E — Epileptic; I — Insane; Sy — Syphilitic; Sx — Sexually immoral; T — Tuberculous.

A short vertical line dependent from the horizontal fraternity line indicates a child whose sex is unknown. An F at the end of the line indicates that such child was feeble-minded.

N ? or F ? indicates that the individual has not been definitely determined, but, considering all the data, it is concluded that on the whole, the person was probably normal or feeble-minded, as the letter signifies.

A small d. followed by a numeral means died at that age; b. means born, usually followed by the date.

A single figure below a symbol indicates that the symbol stands for more than one individual — the number denoted by the figure, *e.g.* a circle with a "4" below it, indicates that there were four girls in that fraternity, represented by that one symbol.

THE CHARTS

The Hand indicates the child that is in the Institution at Vineland, whose family history is the subject of the chart.

A black horizontal line under a symbol indicates that that individual was in some public institution at state expense.

The fact that the parents were not married is indicated either by the expression "unmarried" or by the word "illegitimate," placed near the symbol for the child.

CHART I.

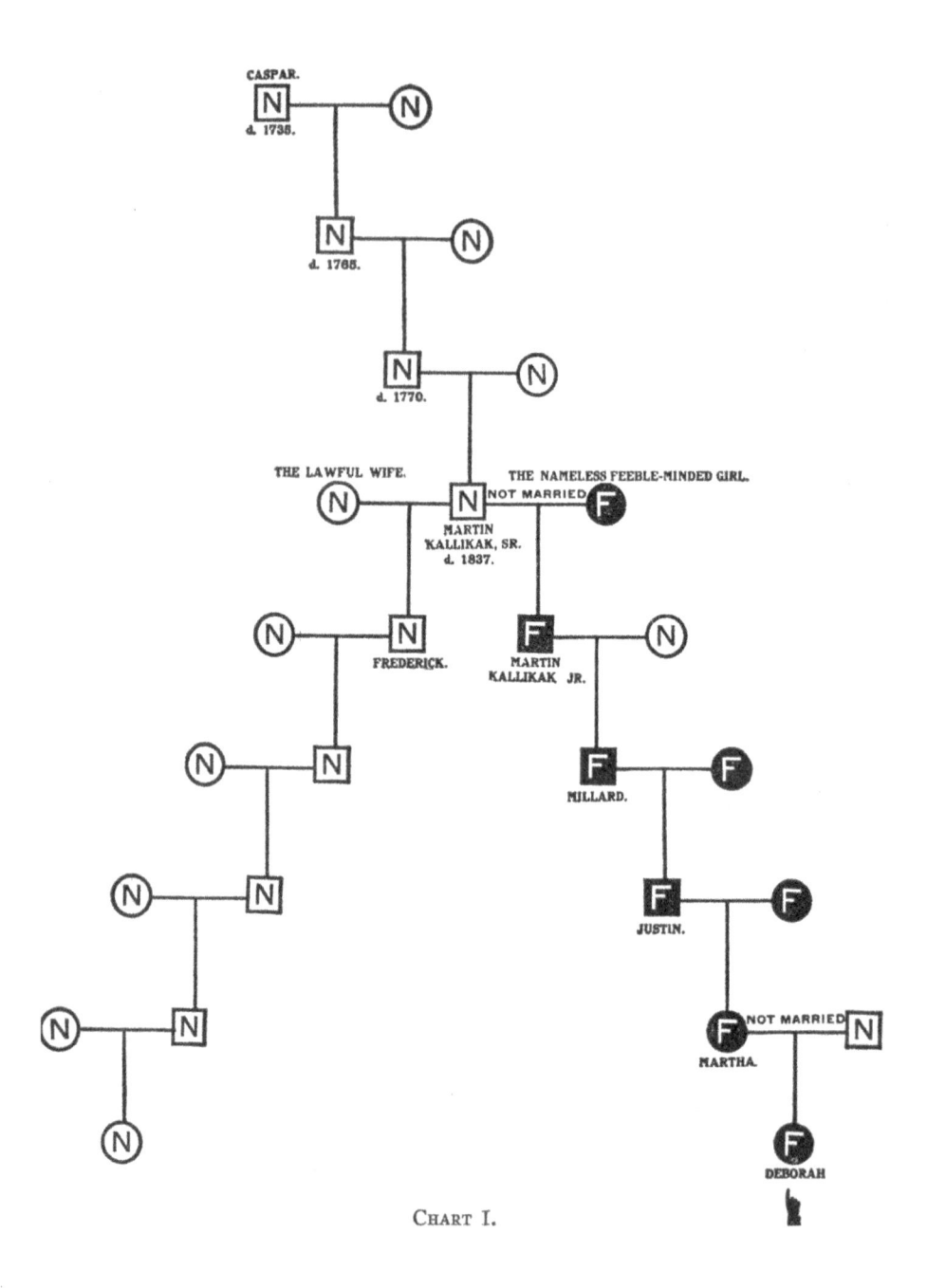

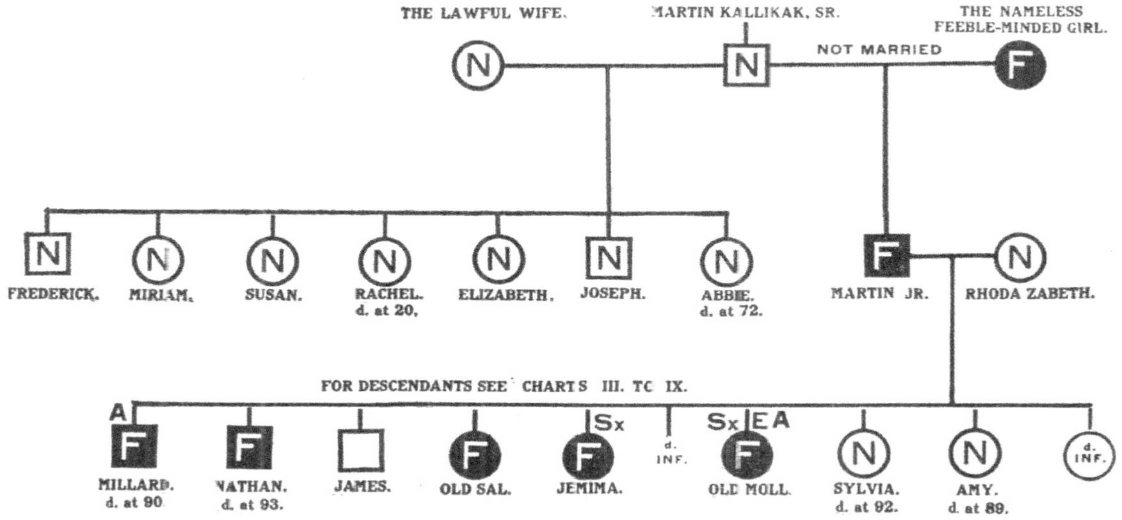

CHART II.

N = Normal. F = Feeble-minded. Sx = Sexually immoral. A = Alcoholic. I = Insane. Sy = Syphilitic. C = Criminalistic. D = Deaf. d. inf. = died in infancy. T = Tuberculous. Hand points to child in Vineland Institution. For further explanation see pp. 33-35.

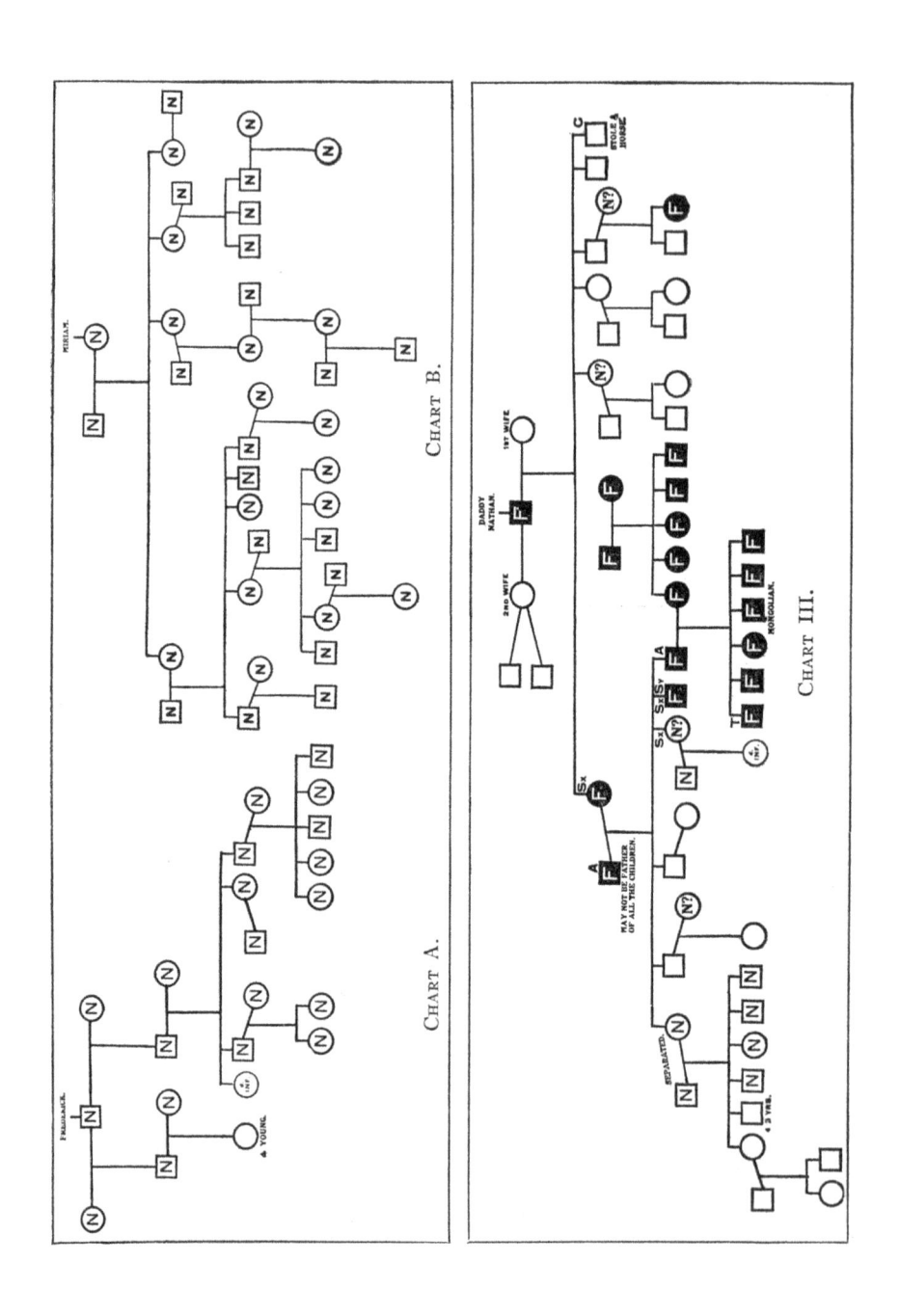

CHART A.

CHART B.

CHART III.

52

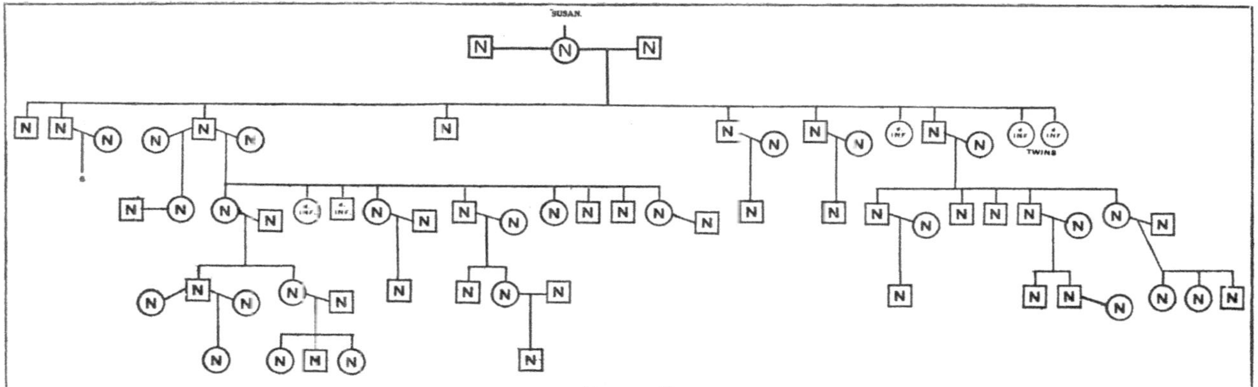

CHART C.

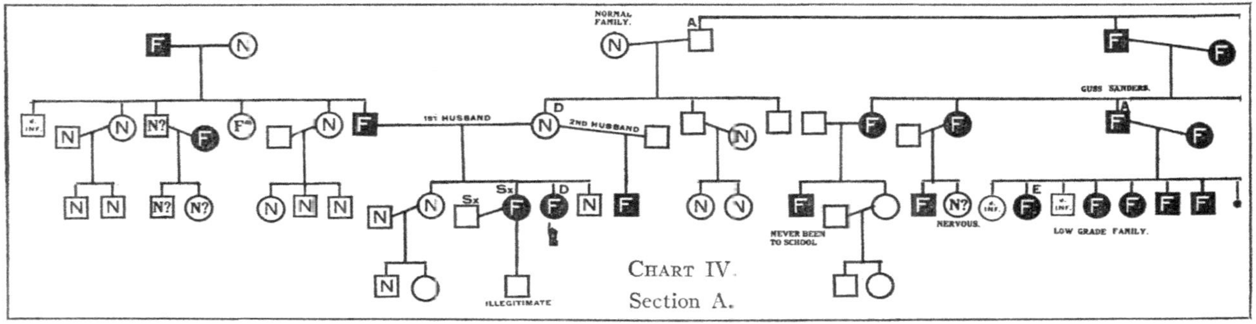

CHART IV.
Section A.

N = Normal. F = Feeble-minded. Sx = Sexually immoral. A = Alcoholic. I = Insane. Sy = Syphilitic. C = Criminalistic. D = Deaf.
d. inf. = died in infancy. T = Tuberculous. Hand points to child in Vineland Institution. For further explanation see pp. 33-35.

53

CHART D.

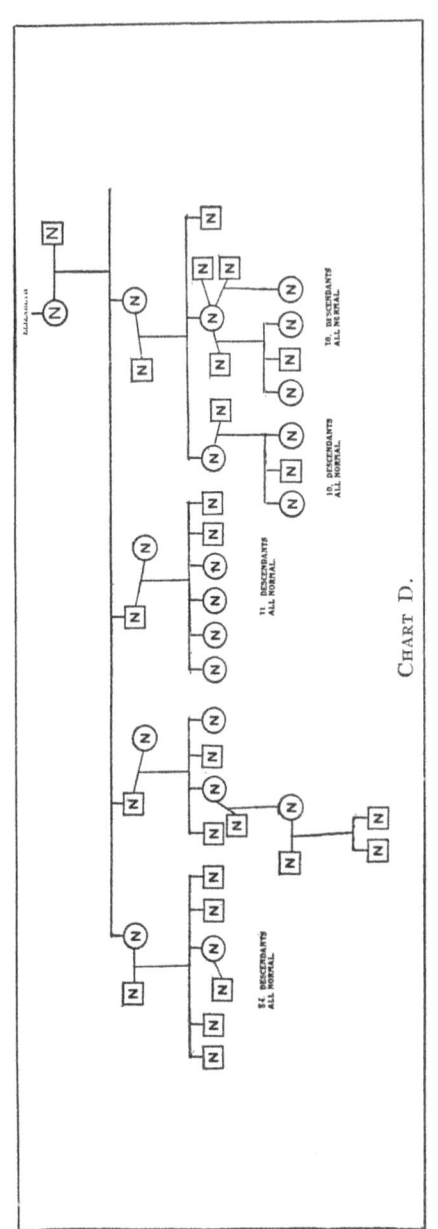

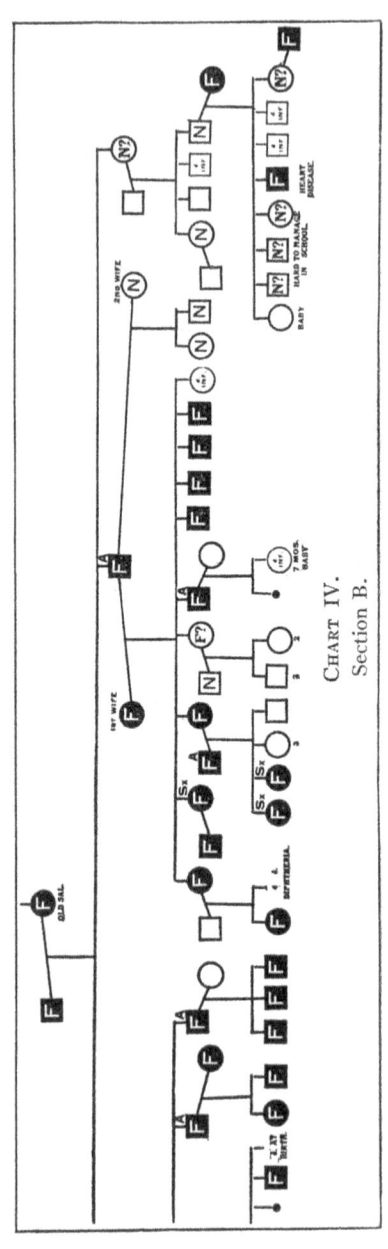

CHART IV.
Section B.

54

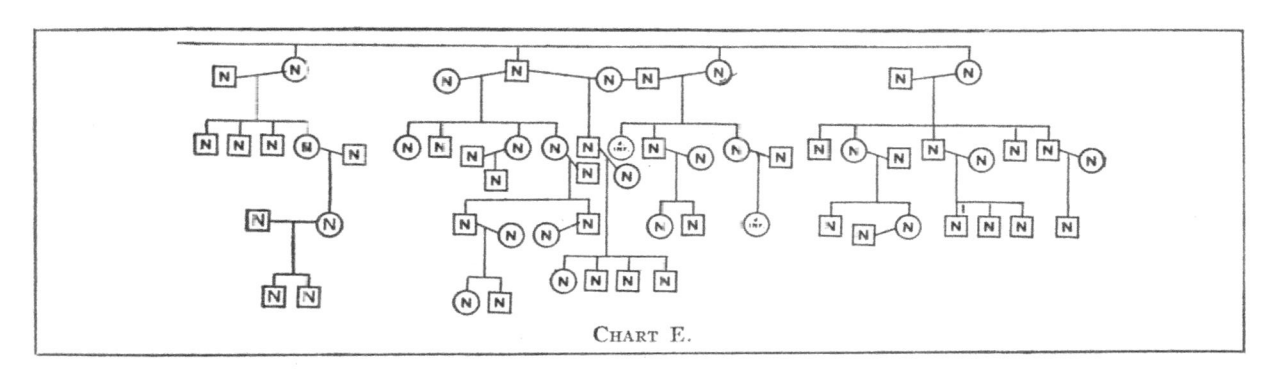

CHART E.

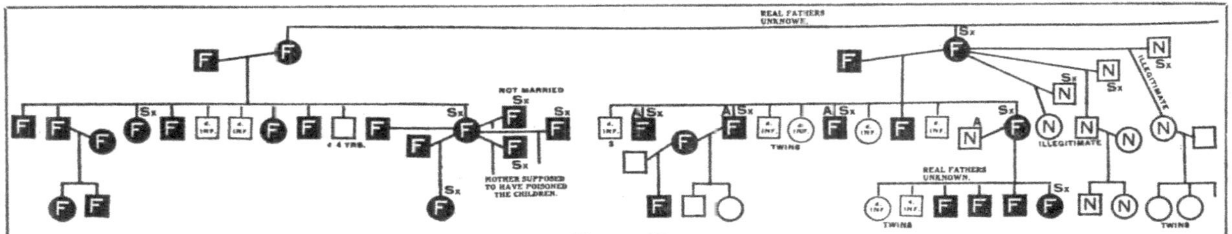

CHART V.
Section A.

N = Normal. F = Feeble-minded. Sx = Sexually immoral. A = Alcoholic. I = Insane. Sy = Syphilitic. C = Criminalistic. D = Deaf. d. inf. = died in infancy. T = Tuberculous. Hand points to child in Vineland Institution. For further explanation see pp. 33–35.

Chart F.

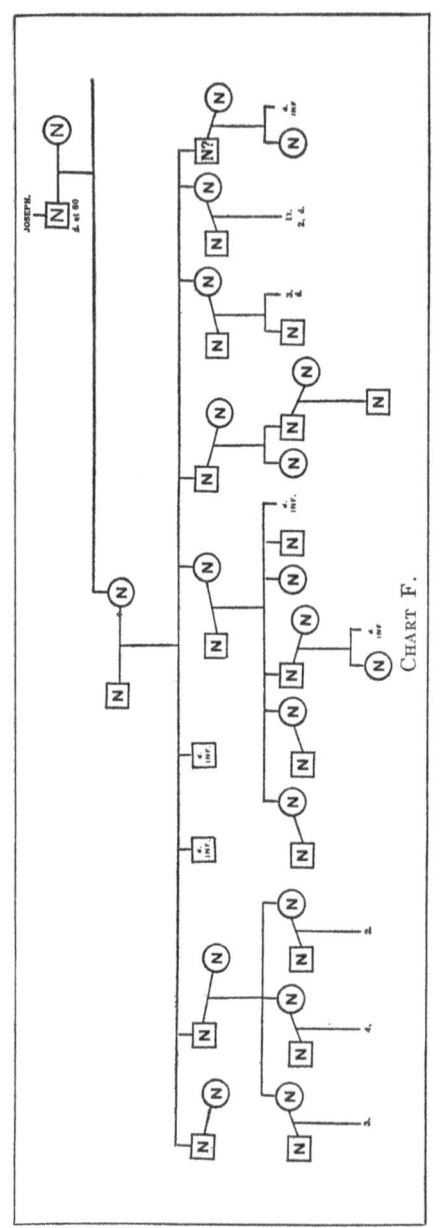

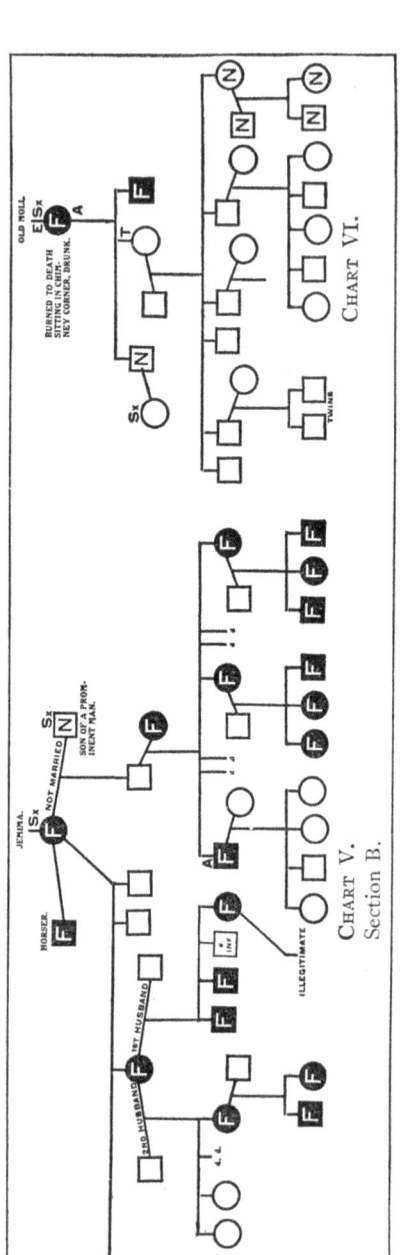

Chart V. Section B.

Chart VI.

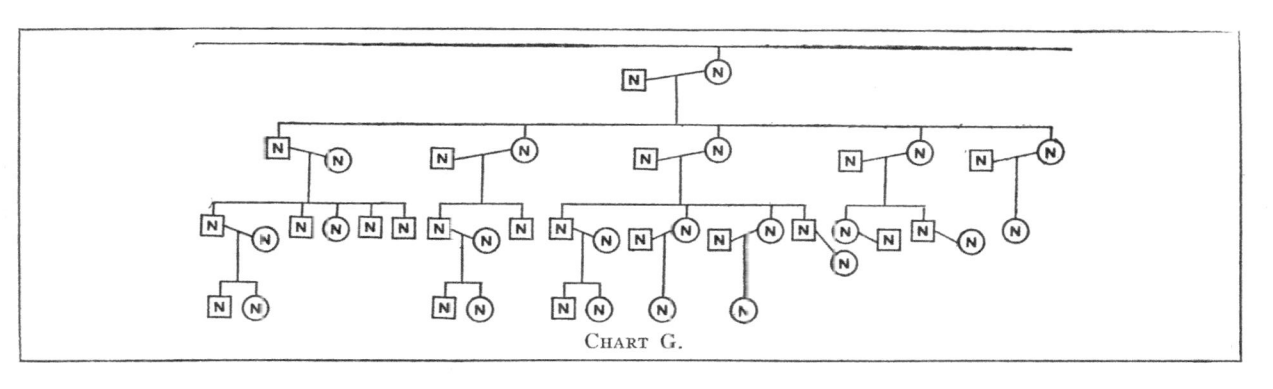

CHART G.

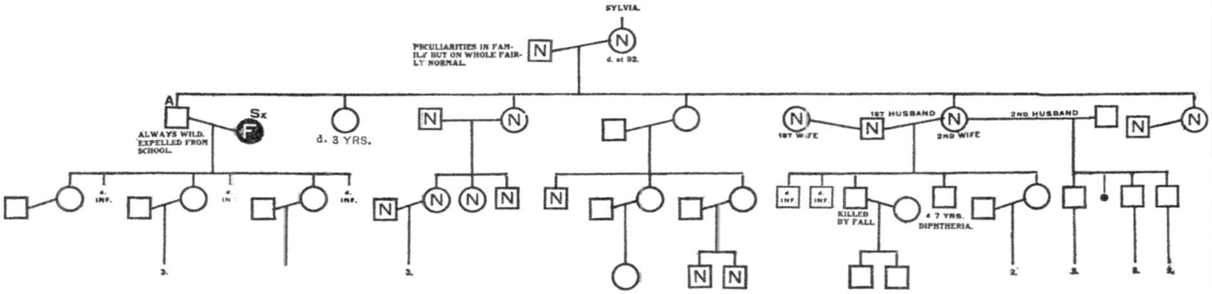

CHART VII.

N = Normal. F = Feeble-minded. Sx = Sexually immoral. A = Alcoholic. I = Insane. Sy = Syphilitic. C = Criminalistic. D = Deaf.
d. inf. = died in infancy. T = Tuberculous. Hand points to child in Vineland Institution. For further explanation see pp. 33–35.

CHART H.

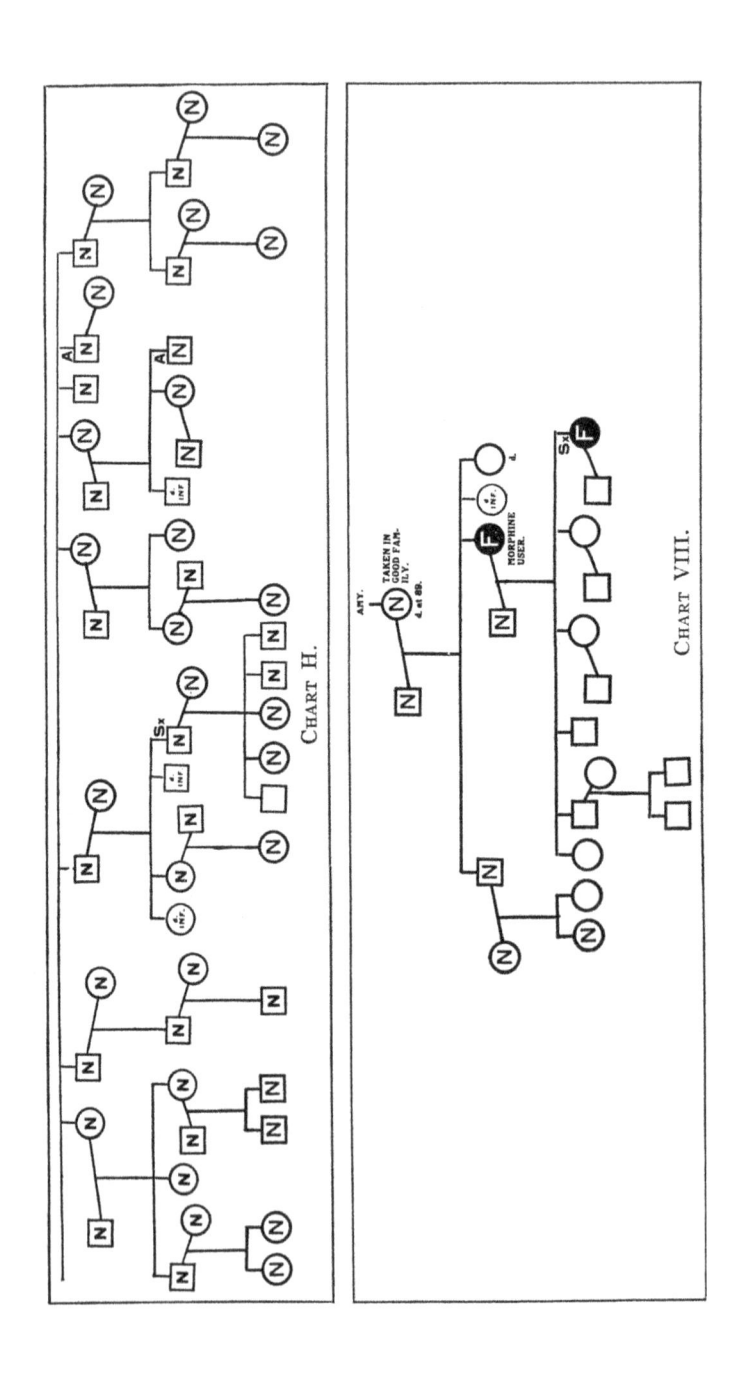

CHART VIII.

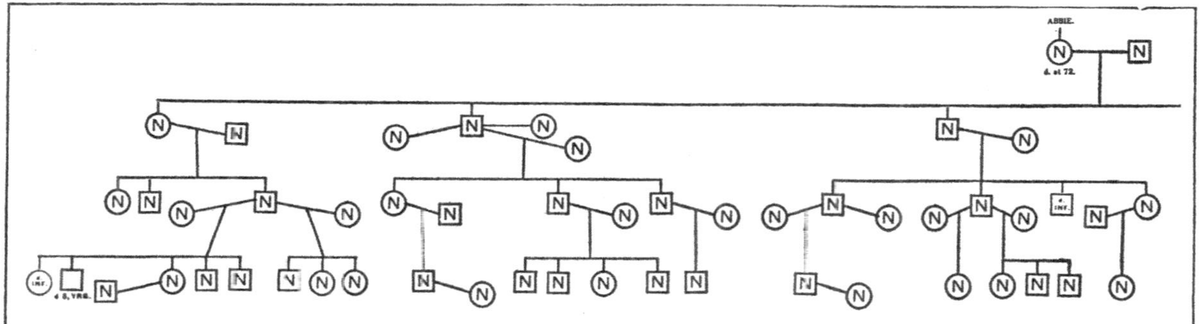

CHART I.

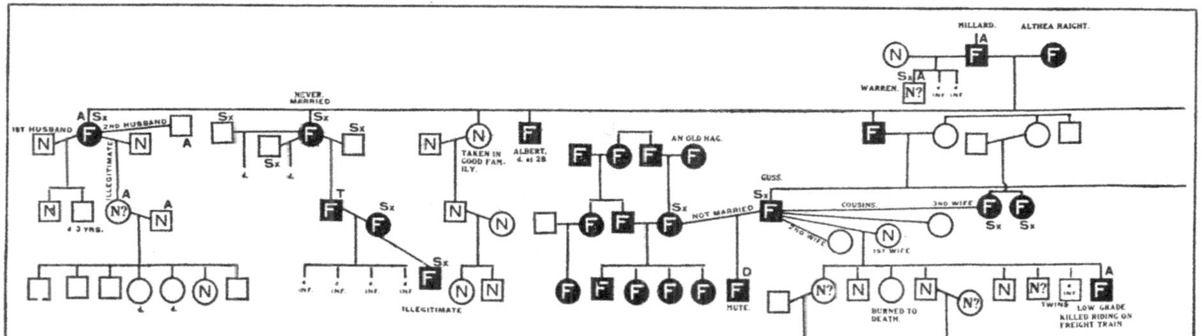

CHART IX.
Section A.

N = Normal. F = Feeble-minded. Sx = Sexually immoral. A = Alcoholic. I = Insane. Sy = Syphilitic. C = Criminalistic. D = Deaf.
d. inf. = die in infancy. T = Tuberculous. Hand points to child in Vineland Institution. For further explanation see pp. 33–35.

CHART J.

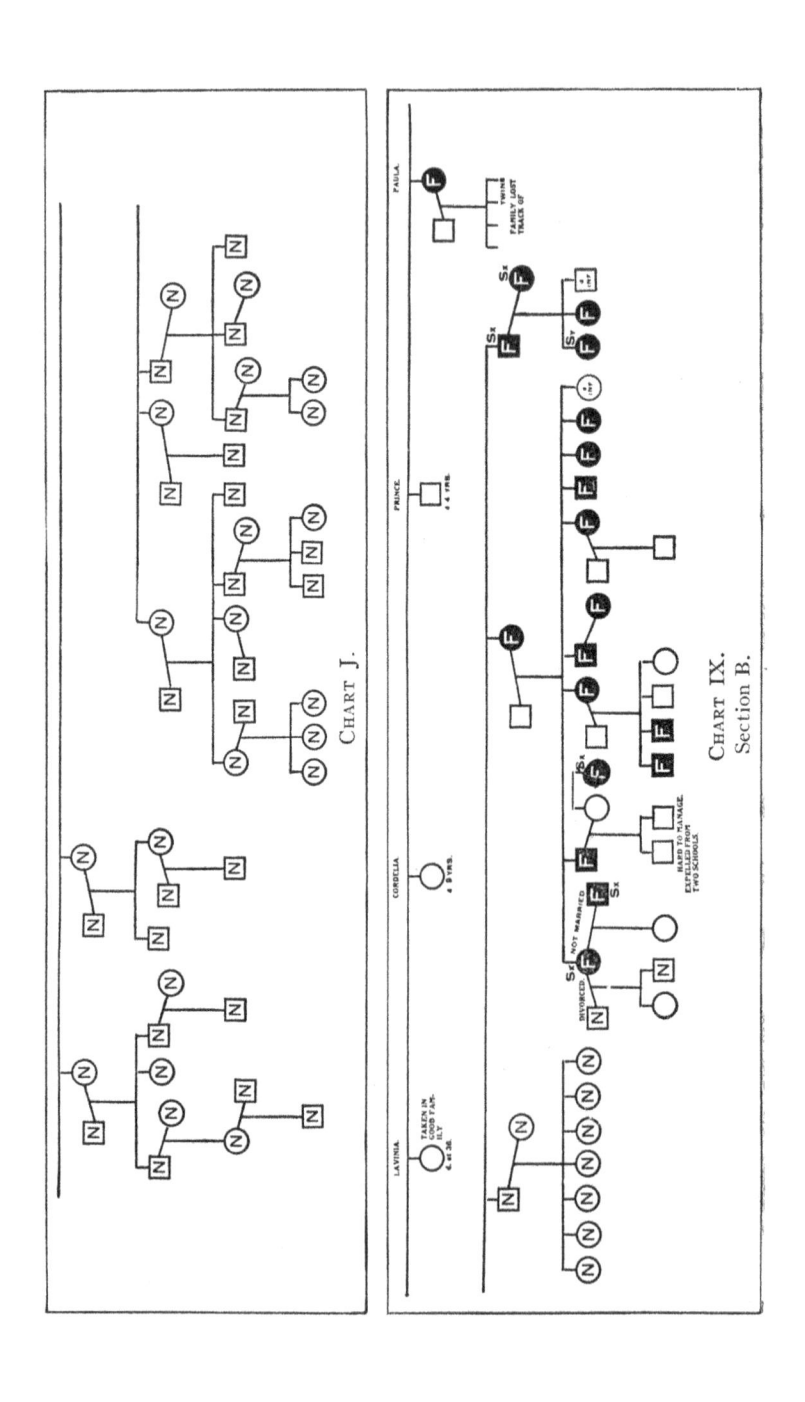

CHART IX.
Section B.

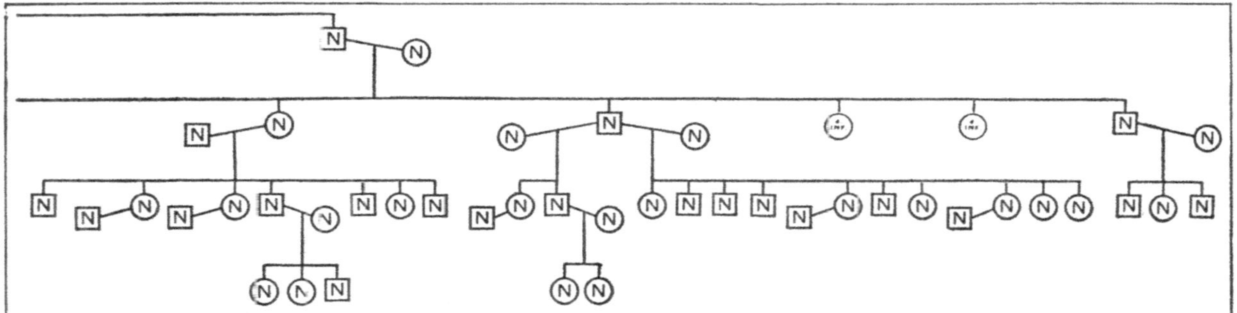

CHART K.

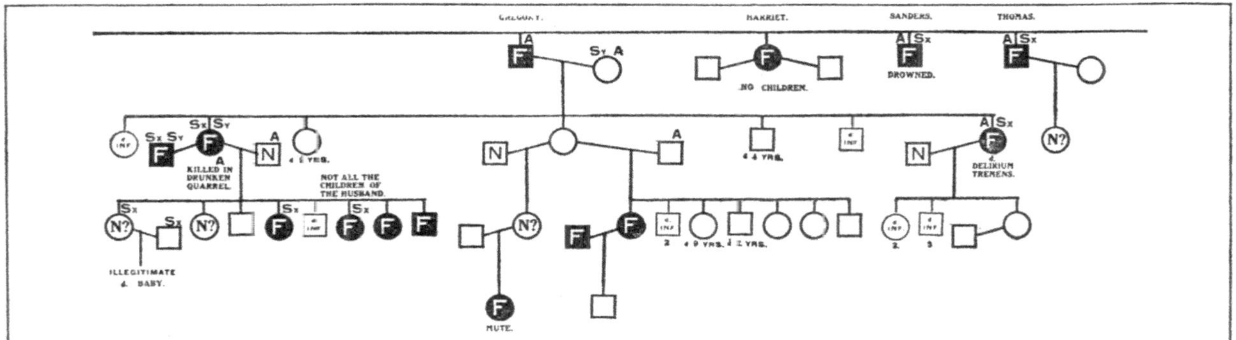

CHART IX.
Section C.

N = Normal. F = Feeble-minded. Sx = Sexually immoral. A = Alcoholic. I = Insane. Sy = Syphilitic. C = Criminalistic. D = Deaf.
d. inf. = died in infancy. T = Tuberculous. Hand points to child in Vineland Institution. For further explanation see pp. 33-35.

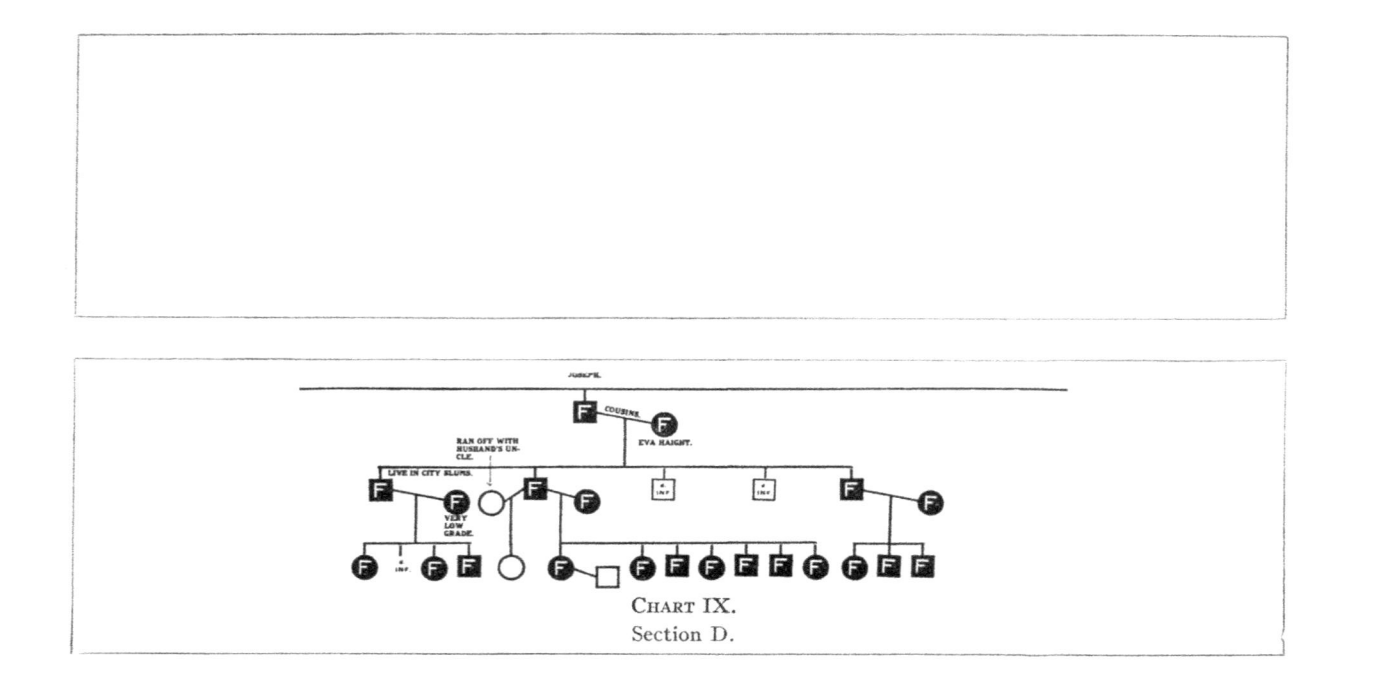

CHART IX.
Section D.

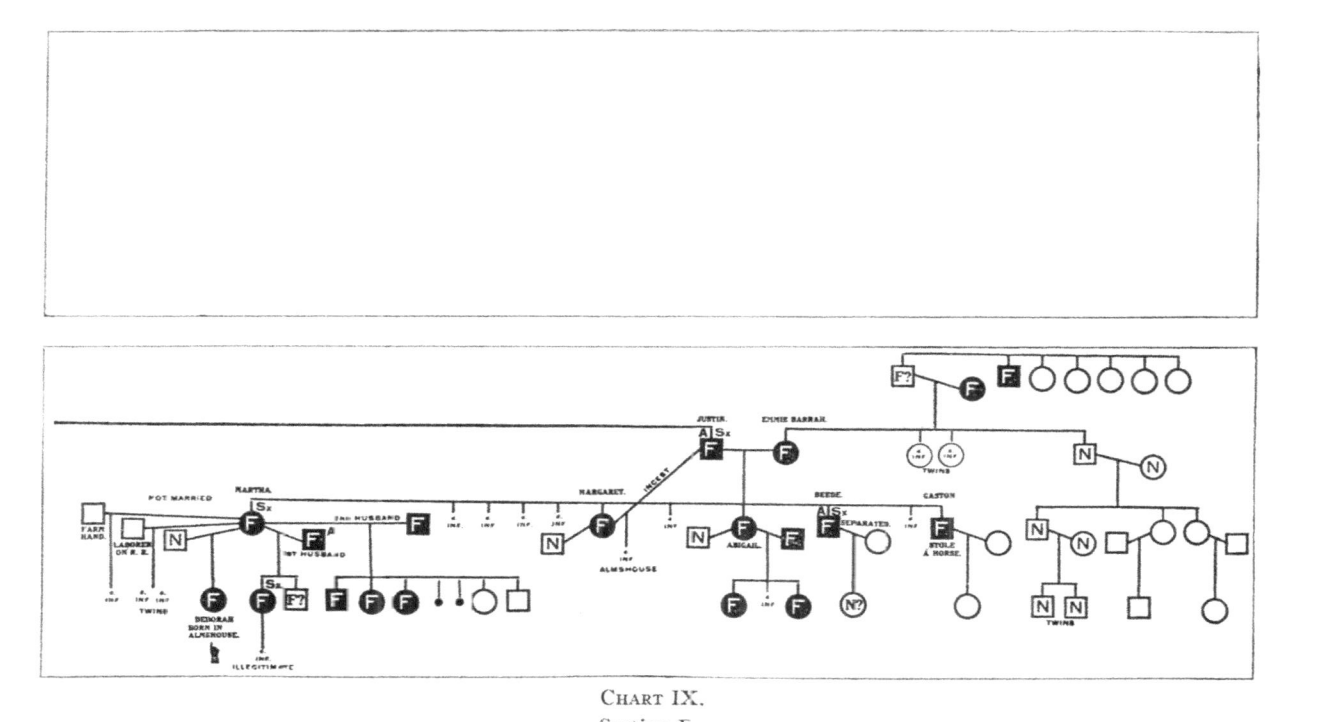

CHART IX.
Section E.

N = Normal. F = Feeble-minded. Sx = Sexually immoral. A = Alcoholic. I = Insane. Sy = Syphilitic. C = Criminalistic. D = Deaf. d. inf. = died in infancy. T = Tuberculous. Hand points to child in Vineland Institution. For further explanation see pp. 33-35.

Chapter III

What it Means

The foregoing charts and text tell a story as instructive as it is amazing. We have here a family of good English blood of the middle class, settling upon the original land purchased from the proprietors of the state in Colonial times, and throughout four generations maintaining a reputation for honor and respectability of which they are justly proud. Then a scion of this family, in an unguarded moment, steps aside from the paths of rectitude and with the help of a feeble-minded girl, starts a line of mental defectives that is truly appalling. After this mistake, he returns to the traditions of his family, marries a woman of his own quality, and through her carries on a line of respectability equal to that of his ancestors.

We thus have two series from two different mothers but the same father. These extend for six generations. Both lines live out their lives in practically the same region and in the same environment, except in so far as they themselves, because of their different characters, changed that environment. Indeed, so close are they that in one case, a defective man on the bad side of the family was found in the employ of a family on the normal side and, although they are of the same name, neither suspects any relationship.

We thus have a natural experiment of remarkable value to the sociologist and the student of heredity. That we are dealing with a problem of true heredity, no one can doubt, for, although of the descendants of Martin Kallikak Jr. many married into feeble-minded families and thus brought in more bad blood, yet Martin Jr. himself married a normal woman, thus demonstrating that the defect is transmitted through the father, at least in this generation. Moreover, the Kallikak family traits appear continually even down to the present generation, and there are many qualities that are alike in both the good and the bad families, thus showing the strength and persistence of the ancestral stock.

The reader will recall the famous story of the Jukes family published by Richard L. Dugdale in 1877, a startling array of criminals, paupers, and diseased persons, more or less related to each other and extending over seven generations.

Dr. Winship has undertaken to compare this family with the descendants of Jonathan Edwards, and from this comparison to draw certain conclusions. It is a striking comparison, but unfortunately not as conclusive as we need in these days. The two families were utterly independent, of different ancestral stock, reared in different communities, even in different States, and under utterly different environment.

The one, starting from a strong, religious, and highly educated ancestor, has maintained those traits and traditions down to the present day and with remarkable results; the other, starting without any of these advantages, and under an entirely different environment, has resulted in the opposite kind of descendants.

It is not possible to convince the euthenist (who holds that environment is the sole factor) that, had the children of Jonathan Edwards and the children of "Old Max" changed places, the results would not have been such as to show that it was a question of environment and not of heredity. And he cites to us the fact that many children of highly developed parents degenerate and become paupers and criminals, while on the other hand, some children born of lowly and even criminal parents take the opposite course and become respectable and useful citizens.

In as far as the children of "Old Max" were of normal mentality, it is not possible to say what might not have become of them, had they had good training and environment.

Fortunately for the cause of science, the Kallikak family, in the persons of Martin Kallikak Jr. and his descendants, are not open to this argument. They were feeble-minded, and no amount of education or good environment can change a feeble-minded individual into a normal one, any more than it can change a red-haired stock into a black-haired stock. The striking fact of the enormous proportion of feeble-minded individuals in the descendants of Martin Kallikak Jr. and the total absence of such in the descendants of his half brothers and sisters is conclusive on this point. Clearly it was not environment that has made that good family. They made their environment; and their own good blood, with the good blood in the families into which they married, told.

So far as the Jukes family is concerned, there is nothing that proves the hereditary character of any of the crime, pauperism, or prostitution that was found. The most that one can say is that if such a family is allowed to go on and develop in its own way unmolested, it is pretty certain not to improve, but rather to propagate its own kind and fill the world with degenerates of one form or another. The formerly much discussed question of the hereditary character of crime received no solution from the Jukes family, but in the light of present-day knowledge of the sciences of criminology and biology, there is every reason to conclude that criminals are made and not born. The best material out of which to make criminals, and perhaps the material from which they are most frequently made, is feeble-mindedness.

The reader must remember that the type of feeble-mindedness of which we are speaking is the one to which Deborah belongs, that is, to the high grade, or moron. All the facts go to show that this type of people makes up a large percentage of our criminals. We may argue a priori that such would be the case. Here we have a group who, when children in school, cannot learn the things that are given them to learn, because through their mental defect, they are incapable of mastering abstractions. They never learn to read sufficiently well to make reading pleasurable or of practical use to them. The same is true of number work. Under our compulsory school system and our present courses of study, we compel these children to go to school, and attempt to teach them the three R's, and even higher subjects. Thus they worry along through a few grades until they are fourteen years old and then leave school, not having learned anything of value or that can help them to make even a meager living in the world. They are then turned out inevitably dependent upon others. A few have relatives who take care of them, see that they learn to do something which perhaps will help in their support, and then these relatives supplement this with enough to insure them a living.

A great majority, however, having no such interested or capable relatives, become at once a direct burden upon society. These divide according to temperament into two groups. Those who are phlegmatic, sluggish, indolent, simply lie down and would starve to death, if some one did not help them. When they come to the attention of our charitable organizations, they are picked up and sent to the almshouse, if they cannot be made to work. The other type is of the nervous, excitable, irritable kind who try to make a living, and not being able to do it by a fair day's work and honest wages, attempt to succeed through dishonest methods. "Fraud is the force of weak natures." These become the criminal type. The kind of criminality into which they fall seems to depend largely upon their environment. If they are associated with vicious but intelligent people, they become the dupes for carrying out any of the hazardous schemes that their more intelligent associates plan for them. Because of their stupidity, they are very apt to be caught quickly and sent to the reformatory or prison. If they are girls, one of the easiest things for them to fall into is a life of prostitution, because they have natural instincts with no power of control and no intelligence to understand the wiles and schemes of the white slaver, the cadet, or the individual seducer. All this, we say, is what is to be expected. These are the people of good outward appearance, but of low intelligence, who pass through school without acquiring any efficiency, then go out into the world and must inevitably fall into some such life as we have pictured.

Let us now turn to our public institutions. These have not yet been sufficiently investigated, nor have we adequate statistics to show what percentage of their inmates is actually feeble-minded. But even casual observation of our almshouse population shows the majority to be of decidedly low mentality, while careful tests would undoubtedly increase this percentage very materially.

In our insane hospitals may also be found a group of people whom the physicians will tell you are only partially demented. The fact is they properly belong in an institution for feeble-minded, rather than in one for the insane, and have gotten into the latter because an unenlightened public does not recognize the difference between a person who has lost his mind and one who never had one.

In regard to criminality, we now have enough studies to make us certain that at least 25 per cent of this class is feeble-minded.

One hundred admissions to the Railway Reformatory, taken in order of admission, show at least 26 per cent of them distinctly feeble-minded, with the certainty that the percentage would be much higher if we included the border-line cases.

An investigation of one hundred of the Juvenile Court children in the Detention Home of the City of Newark showed that 67 per cent of them were distinctly feeble-minded. From this estimate are excluded children who are yet too young for us to know definitely whether the case is one of arrested development. This point once determined would unquestionably swell the percentage of defect.

An examination of fifty-six girls from a Massachusetts reformatory, but out on probation, showed that fifty-two of them were distinctly feeble-minded. This was partially a selected group, the basis being their troublesomeness; they were girls who could not be made to stay in the homes that were found for them, nor to do reasonable and sensible things in those homes, which fact, of itself, pointed toward feeble-mindedness.

The foregoing are figures based on actual test examinations as to mental capacity. If we accept the estimates of the mental condition of the inmates made by the superintendents of reformatories and penal institutions, we get sometimes a vastly higher percentage; *e.g.* the Superintendent of the Elmira Reformatory estimates that at least 40 per cent of his inmates are mental defectives.

Indeed, it would not be surprising if careful examination of the inmates of these institutions should show that even 50 per cent of them are distinctly feeble-minded.

In regard to prostitutes, we have no reliable figures. The groups of delinquent girls to which we have already referred included among the numbers several that were already known as prostitutes. A simple observation of persons who are leading this sort of life will satisfy any one who is familiar with feeble-mindedness that a large percentage of them actually are defective mentally. So we have, as is claimed, partly from statistical studies and partly from careful observation, abundant evidence of the truth of our claim that criminality is often made out of feeble-mindedness.

Mr. Winship in his comparison of the Jukes and Edwards families has strengthened our claim in this respect. In all environments and under all conditions, he shows the latter family blossoming out into distinguished citizens, not primarily through anything from without but through the imperious force within. Since we may conclude that none of the Edwards family, who are described by Dr. Winship, were feeble-minded, therefore none of them became criminals or prostitutes. But here again his argument is inconclusive because he does not tell us of all the descendants.

With equal safety it may be surmised that many of the Jukes family (perhaps the original stock, indeed) were feeble-minded and therefore easily lapsed into the kind of lives that they are said to have lived.

In the good branch of the Kallikak family there were no criminals. There were not many in the other side, but there were some, and, had their environment been different, no one who is familiar with feeble-minded persons, their characteristics and tendencies, would doubt that a large percentage of them might have become criminal. Lombroso's famous criminal types, in so far as they were types, may have been types of feeble-mindedness on which criminality was grafted by the circumstances of their environment.

Such facts as those revealed by the Kallikak family drive us almost irresistibly to the conclusion that before we can settle our problems of criminality and pauperism and all the rest of the social problems that are taxing our time and money, the first and fundamental step should be to decide upon the mental capacity of the persons who make up these groups. We must separate, as sharply as possible, those persons who are weak-minded, and therefore irresponsible, from intelligent criminals. Both our method of treatment and our attitude towards crime will be changed when we discover what part of this delinquency is due to irresponsibility.

If the Jukes family were of normal intelligence, a change of environment would have worked wonders and would have saved society from the horrible blot. But if they were feeble-minded, then no amount of good environment could have made them anything else than feeble-minded. Schools and colleges were not for them, rather a segregation which would have prevented them from falling into evil and from procreating their kind, so avoiding the transmitting of their defects and delinquencies to succeeding generations.

Thus where the Jukes-Edwards comparison is weak and the argument inconclusive, the twofold Kallikak family is strong and the argument convincing.

Environment does indeed receive some support from three cases in our chart. On Chart II, two children of Martin Jr. and Rhoda were normal, while all the rest were feeble-minded. It is true that here one parent was normal, and we have the right to expect some normal children. At the same time, these were the two children that were adopted into good families and brought up under good surroundings. They proved to be normal and their descendants normal. Again, on Chart IX-a, we have one child of two feeble-minded parents who proves to be normal — the only one among the children. This child was also taken into a good family and brought up carefully. Another sister (Chart IX-b) was also taken into a good family and, while not determined, yet "showed none of the traits that are usually indicative of feeble-mindedness." It may be claimed that environment is responsible for this good result. It is certainly significant that the only children in these families that were normal, or at least better than the rest, were brought up in good families.

However, it would seem to be rather dangerous to base any very positive hope on environment in the light of these charts, taken as a whole. There are too many other possible explanations of the anomaly, *e.g.* these cases may have been high-grade morons, who, to the untrained person, would seem so nearly normal, that at this late day it would be impossible to find any one who would remember their traits well enough to enable us to classify them as morons.

We must not forget that, on Chart IX-e, we also have the daughter of Justin taken into a good family and carefully brought up, but in spite of all that, she proved to be feebleminded. The same is probably true of Deborah's half brother.

We have claimed that criminality resulting from feeblemindedness is mainly a matter of environment, yet it must be acknowledged that there are wide differences in temperament and that, while this one branch of the Kallikak family was mentally defective, there was no strong tendency in it towards that which our laws recognize as criminality. In other families there is, without doubt, a much greater tendency to crime, so that the lack of criminals in this particular case, far from detracting from our argument, really strengthens it. It must be recognized that there is much more liability of criminals resulting from mental defectiveness in certain families than in others, probably because of difference in the strength of some instincts.

This difference in temperament is perhaps nowhere better brought out than in the grandparents of Deborah. The grandfather belonging to the Kallikak family had the temperament and characteristics of that family, which, while they did not lead him into positive criminality of high degree, nevertheless did make him a bad man of a positive type, a drunkard, a sex pervert, and all that goes to make up a bad character.

On the other hand, his wife and her family were simply stupid, with none of the pronounced tendencies to evil that were shown in the Kallikak family. They were not vicious, nor given over to bad practices of any sort. But they were inefficient, without power to get on in the world, and they transmitted these qualities to their descendants.

Thus, of the children of this pair, the grandparents of Deborah, the sons have been active and positive in their lives, the one being a horse thief, the other a sexual pervert, having the alcoholic tendency of his father, while the daughters are quieter and more passive. Their dullness, however, does not amount to imbecility. Deborah's mother herself was of a high type of moron, with a certain quality which carried with it an element of refinement. Her sister was the passive victim of her father's incestuous practice and later married a normal man. Another sister was twice married, the first time through the agency of the good woman who attended to the legalizing of Deborah's mother's alliances, the last time, the man, being normal, attended to this himself. He was old and only wanted a housekeeper, and this woman, having been strictly raised in an excellent family, was famous as a cook, so this arrangement seemed to him best. None of these sisters ever objected to the marriage ceremony when the matter was attended to for them, but they never seem to have thought of it as necessary when living with any man.

The stupid helplessness of Deborah's mother in regard to her own impulses is shown by the facts of her life. Her first child had for its father a farm hand; the father of the second and third (twins) was a common laborer on the railroad. Deborah's father was a young fellow, normal indeed, but loose in his morals, who, along with others, kept company with the mother while she was out at service. After Deborah's birth in the almshouse, the mother had been taken with her child into a good family. Even in this guarded position, she was sought out by a feeble-minded man of low habits. Every possible means was employed to separate the pair, but without effect. Her mistress then insisted that they marry, and herself attended to all the details. After Deborah's mother had borne this man two children, the pair went to live on the farm of an unmarried man possessing some property, but little intelligence. The husband was an imbecile who had never provided for his wife. She was still pretty, almost girlish — the farmer was good-looking, and soon the two were openly living together and the husband had left. As the facts became known, there was considerable protest in the neighborhood, but no active steps were taken until two or three children had been born. Finally, a number of leading citizens, headed by the good woman before alluded to, took the matter up in earnest. They found the husband and persuaded him to allow them to get him a divorce. Then they compelled the farmer to marry the woman. He agreed, on condition that the children which were not his should be sent away. It was at this juncture that Deborah was brought to the Training School.

In visiting the mother in her present home and in talking with her over different phases of her past life, several things are evident; there has been no malice in her life nor voluntary reaction against social order, but simply a blind following of impulse which never rose to objective consciousness. Her life has utterly lacked coordination — there has been no reasoning from cause to effect, no learning of any lesson. She has never known shame; in a word, she has never struggled and never suffered. Her husband is a selfish, sullen, penurious person who gives his wife but little money, so that she often resorts to selling soap and other things among her neighbors to have something to spend. At times she works hard in the field as a farm hand, so that it cannot be wondered at that her house is neglected and her children unkempt. Her philosophy of life is the philosophy of the animal. There is no complaining, no irritation at the inequalities of fate. Sickness, pain, childbirth, death — she accepts them all with the same equanimity as she accepts the opportunity of putting a new dress and a gay ribbon on herself and children and going to a Sunday School picnic. There is no rising to the comprehension of the possibilities which life offers or of directing circumstances to a definite, higher end. She has a certain fondness for her children, but is incapable of real solicitude for them. She speaks of those who were placed in homes and is glad to see their pictures, and has a sense of their belonging to her, but it is faint, remote, and in no way bound up with her life. She is utterly helpless to protect her older daughters, now on the verge of womanhood, from the dangers that beset them, or to inculcate in them any ideas which would lead to self-control or to the directing of their lives in an orderly manner.

The same lack is strikingly shown, if we turn our attention to the question of alcoholism in this family. We learn from a responsible member of the good branch of the family that the appetite for alcoholic stimulants has been strong in the past in this family and that several members in recent generations have been more or less addicted to its use. Only two have actually allowed it to get the better of them to the extent that they became incapacitated. Both were physicians. In the other branch, however, with the weakened mentality, we find twenty-four victims of this habit so pronounced that they were public nuisances. We have taken no account of the much larger number who were also addicted to its use, but who did not become so bad as to be considered alcoholic in our category.

Thus we see that the normal mentality of the good branch of the family was able to cope successfully with this intense thirst, while the weakened mentality on the other side was unable to escape, and many fell victims to this appalling habit.

It is such facts as these, taken as we find them, not only in this family but in many of the other families whose records we are soon to publish, that lead us to the conclusion that drunkenness is, to a certain extent at least, the result of feeble-mindedness and that one way to reduce drunkenness is first to determine the mentally defective people, and save them from the environment which would lead them into this abuse.

Again, eight of the descendants of the degenerate Kallikak branch were keepers of houses of ill fame, and that in spite of the fact that they mostly lived in a rural community where such places do not flourish as they do in large cities.

In short, whereas in the Jukes-Edwards comparison we have no sound basis for argument, because the families were utterly different and separate, in the Kallikak family the conclusion seems thoroughly logical. We have, as it were, a natural experiment with a normal branch with which to compare our defective side. We have the one ancestor giving us a line of normal people that shows thoroughly good all the way down the generations, with the exception of the one man who was sexually loose and the two who gave way to the appetite for strong drink.

This is our norm, our standard, our demonstration of what the Kallikak blood is when kept pure, or mingled with blood as good as its own.

Over against this we have the bad side, the blood of the same ancestor contaminated by that of the nameless feeble-minded girl.

From this comparison the conclusion is inevitable that all this degeneracy has come as the result of the defective mentality

WHAT IT MEANS

and bad blood having been brought into the normal family of good blood, first from the nameless feeble-minded girl and later by additional contaminations from other sources.

The biologist could hardly plan and carry out a more rigid experiment or one from which the conclusions would follow more inevitably.

Chapter IV

Further Facts About the Kallikak Family

ALTHOUGH THE foregoing facts, figures, and charts show conclusively the difference between good heredity and bad and the result of introducing mental deficiency into the family blood, yet because it is so difficult actually to appreciate the situation, because facts and figures do not have flesh and blood reality in them, we give in this chapter a few cases, graphically written up by our field worker, to show the differences in the types of people on the two sides of the family. These are only a few of the many, but are fairly typical of the condition of things that was found throughout the investigation. On the bad side we have the type of family which the social worker meets continually and which makes most of our social problems. A study of it will help to account for the conviction we have that no amount of work in the slums or removing the slums from our cities will ever be successful until we take care of those who make the slums what they are. Unless the two lines of work go on together, either one is bound to be futile in itself. If all of the slum districts of our cities were removed to-morrow and model tenements built in their places, we would still have slums in a week's time, because we have these mentally defective people who can never be taught to live otherwise than as they have been living. Not until we take care of this class and see to it that their lives are guided by intelligent people, shall we remove these sores from our social life.

There are Kallikak families all about us. They are multiplying at twice the rate of the general population, and not until we recognize this fact, and work on this basis, will we begin to solve these social problems.

The following pictures from life have been prepared by our field worker, Miss Elizabeth S. Kite, and besides giving an idea of the family, they will also show something of her method, and enable the reader to judge of the reliability of the data.

On one of the coldest days in winter the field worker visited the street in a city slum where three sons of Joseph (Chart IX, section D) live. She had previously tested several of the children of these families in the public school and found them, in amiability of character and general mentality, strikingly like our own Deborah, lacking, however, her vitality. There was no fire in their eyes, but a languid dreamy look, which was partly due, no doubt, to unwholesome city environment. In one house she found the family group — six human beings, two cats, and two dogs — huddled in a small back room around a cook stove, the only fire in the house. In this room were accumulated all the paraphernalia of living. A boy of eleven, who had been tested in the school previously, was standing by the fire with a swollen face. He had been kept home on this account. In a rocking-chair, a little girl of twelve was holding a pale faced, emaciated baby. In the corner two boys were openly exposing themselves. The mother was making her toilet by the aid of a comb and basin of water, set on the hearth of the stove; a pot and kettle were on top. The entrance of the field worker caused no commotion of any kind. The boy with the swollen face looked up and smiled, the mother smiled and went on with her toilet, the girl with the baby smiled, the boys in the corner paid no attention. A chair was finally cleared off and she sat down, while everybody smiled. She learned that the husband made a dollar a day and that the girl next older than the child of twelve was married and had a baby. Another younger girl was at school, the family having been at last able to provide her with shoes. The girl of twelve should have been at school, according to the law, but when one saw her face, one realized it made no difference. She was pretty, with olive complexion and dark, languid eyes, but there was no mind there. Stagnation was the word written in large characters over everything. Benumbed by this display of human degeneracy, the field worker went out into the icy street.

A short distance farther on, she came to the home of another brother. The hideous picture that presented itself as the door opened to her knock was one never to be forgotten. In the first home, the type was no lower than moron. One felt that when winter was over and spring had come, the family would expand into a certain expression of life — but here, no such outlook was possible, for the woman at the head of this house was an imbecile. In one arm she held a frightful looking baby, while she had another by the hand. Vermin were visible all over her. In the room were a few chairs and a bed, the latter without any washable covering and filthy beyond description. There was no fire, and both mother and babies were thinly clad. They did not shiver, however, nor seem to mind. The oldest girl, a vulgar, repulsive creature of fifteen, came into the room and stood looking at the stranger. She had somehow managed to live. All the rest of the children, except the two that the mother was carrying, had died in infancy.

The following is a story of Guss, whose position will be found on Chart IX, section A.

When young, he married a normal girl who belonged to a decent family, but had no education. After a few months the mother of our Deborah came to visit them. She was then a young girl, ready to associate with any man who would look at her. The two behaved so badly that the wife turned her out. This was the first knowledge the wife had of the character of her husband. She lived with him ten years or more. In that time he did not average three months' work out of twelve, so she had, practically, to support him and her ever increasing family. She knew that he was untrue to her, but there was no way to prove it. At last she seemed to grasp the situation. She began to believe that there was something wrong with him mentally,—wrong with the whole family, — so she decided to leave him. She took her six living children, rented another house and turned him adrift. He went at once to live with a feeble-minded girl belonging to a low-grade family of the neighborhood. Soon after this girl's child was born he left her, becoming promiscuous in his relations. At one time, he and two of his cousins spent the best part of two days and nights in a tree to elude the police, who were searching for them and another man, all of whom had been accused by a girl then in confinement. When the other man was caught and made to marry the girl, they came down.

In 1904, this scion of the Kallikak family, Guss, went off with a gypsy camp and was married to one of the women. For some time he stayed with the camp, following them into another State. In the neighborhood where they located, a murder was committed which was fastened upon the gypsies and finally settled upon him. A great sensation was raised in the papers about it. He was arrested, but finally cleared of the charge, though not until he was effectually cured of his love for gypsy life.

In 1907, — and here comes the most infamous part of the story, — a minister married Guss to his own first cousin, a woman of questionable character. The witnesses were Guss's sister and her husband. Every one concerned, except the minister, knew that around the corner, in a little street, so near that at certain hours of the day the shadow of the church spire under which they were standing fell upon it, was a house in which Guss's lawful wife was living and working to support his children. The minister, too, might have known, had he taken the least trouble, and thus have been spared the ignominy of uniting two such beings with this travesty of the blessing of heaven. Soon after their union, this couple ceased to live together — Guss going off with another woman and his wife with another man.

The field worker was not able to locate Guss, but she found that a minister farther up the State had, in 1910, married his late wife to the man with whom she was living. The couple, however, had gotten wind that some one was looking for them, so when the field worker arrived, she found that they had moved on, leaving no address.

The following story shows the continuation of these conditions into the next generation: —

It was considered desirable to see the illegitimate son of Guss, who had been born to the feeble-minded girl after Guss had been turned adrift by his lawful wife. This child had had, when young, a severe attack of scarlet fever which deprived him of his hearing. He had been admitted into a home for deaf children, but the mother had taken him out. It was learned that this girl had married her own cousin and that the pair were living on the outskirts of a country town, with this deaf boy and four of their own children.

Arrived at this place, the field worker first sought the school where these children were supposed to go, hoping to obtain some light on the question of their mentality and also to learn their school record. She found that they so seldom attended school that the teacher could give very little information regarding them. By dint of persistent inquiry, the family was discovered living in the back shed of a dilapidated country tenement.

It was a bitter, cold day in February and about eleven in the morning when the field worker knocked at the door. Used as she was to sights of misery and degradation, she was hardly prepared for the spectacle within. The father, a strong, healthy, broad-shouldered man, was sitting helplessly in a corner. The mother, a pretty woman still, with remnants of ragged garments drawn about her, sat in a chair, the picture of despondency. Three children, scantily clad and with shoes that would barely hold together, stood about with drooping jaws and the unmistakable look of the feeble-minded. Another child, neither more intelligent nor better clad, was attempting to wash a few greasy dishes in cold water. The deaf boy was nowhere to be seen. On being urgently requested, the mother went out of the room to get him, for he was not yet out of bed. In a few moments she returned. The boy with her wore an old suit that evidently was made to do service by night as well as by day. A glance sufficed to establish his mentality, which was low. The whole family was a living demonstration of the futility of trying to make desirable citizens from defective stock through making and enforcing compulsory education laws. Here were children who seldom went to school because they seldom had shoes, but when they went, had neither will nor power to learn anything out of books. The father himself, though strong and vigorous, showed by his face that he had only a child's mentality. The mother in her filth and rags was also a child. In this house of abject poverty, only one sure prospect was ahead, that it would produce more feeble-minded children with which to clog the wheels of human progress. The laws of the country will not permit children ten years old to marry. Why should they permit it when the mentality is only ten? These and similar questions kept ringing through the field worker's mind as she made her way laboriously over the frozen road to the station.

Early in the course of this investigation, it had been learned that the father of Deborah's mother had come, when a young man, to the prosperous rural community where his daughter was living at the time of our investigation. The informant could not say whence he had come, but the name of a person was given who was supposed to know. Many fruitless attempts to find this person were made before the object was attained. When at last discovered, she turned out to be an elderly lady of refinement and culture. Strangely enough, long afterwards it was learned that she was connected with the good side of the Kallikak family, but was all unconscious of the relationship which existed between it and the degenerate branch. She was delighted to go back in memory and recall impressions made on her mind in youth.

She had been raised in B—, a town at the foot of a mountain chain upon whose top the grandfather of Deborah's grandfather, Martin Kallikak Jr., had always lived. When she was a little girl, he was a very old man. She remembered being taken to drive, when a child, and seeing the old hut on the mountain, where he lived with his strange daughters, "Old Moll," "Old Sall," and Jemima. The dilapidated dwelling, with its windows bulging with rags, formed a picture she had never forgotten. There were in her mind floating memories of great scandals connected with these women and their lonely mountain hut. The father went by the name of the "Old Horror," and as she remembered him, he was always unwashed and drunk. At election time, he never failed to appear in somebody's cast-off clothing, ready to vote, for the price of a drink, the donor's ticket.

This information, coming when it did, seemed amazing and carried with it the probability of establishing the certainty of defect transmitted through five generations. But the town in question was remote and the probability of finding any living person able to give accurate information seemed so slight that nothing further was done in this direction for many months.

In the meantime, the families of the fifteen brothers and sisters of Deborah's grandfather had been worked out, and the names of several living relatives back in the mountain ascertained. The time was ripe.

Appealing for a night's lodging at the home of a retired farmer, the field worker was fortunate enough to be received. As the hostess was showing her to a room, she asked tentatively, "You have lived in B— a long time?" "About sixty-five years," was the pleasant reply. "So, then, you know something of most of the old families?" "There are not many old residents of B— with whose history I am not familiar." Then followed a few cautious questions in regard to the Kallikak family which drew forth answers that soon convinced the field worker she was on solid ground and could advance without wasting time in needless precautions. At this juncture, the supper bell rang. In the dining room the acquaintance of the host was made. When the meal was over, the couple turned their united attention to the problem put before them. "Why," the host began, when he comprehended what was wanted, "do you know that is the worst nest you're getting into, in the whole country? The mountains back here are full of these people; I can point out to you where every one of them lives." Then he turned to the table and began to sketch a map of the mountain roads which must be followed next day. In the midst of this he paused, as though an idea had come to him, then he said hesitatingly, "You see, it's really impossible for a stranger like you to find all these people. Some of them live on obscure back roads that you could hardly get at without a guide. Now, my time is of no value, and if you will permit me, I will gladly serve in that capacity myself." Needless to say, his services were thankfully accepted, with the result that nearly two hundred persons were added to Deborah's family chart.

This proved, however, only the beginning of the study that has been made of the family in the vicinity of B——. Numerous visits to many homes, always from the center of the genial couple's house, have made the field worker such a well-known figure among these people, that they long ago forgot what little surprise they may have felt at her first visit. "You're one of the family?" was frequently asked her at the beginning. "No, not really, only as I know so many of your cousins and aunts and uncles, I thought, since I was in B——, I would like to know you." This usually sufficed, but if it did not, the field worker was able so to inundate the questioner with information about his own relatives, that before she was through, he had forgotten that anything remained unanswered. The relation once established, no further explanation was necessary. She was able to go in and out among them, study their mentality, awake their reminiscences, until finally the whole story was told.

Besides members of the family, numerous old people were here and there discovered who were able to add materially to the information otherwise obtained. One shrewd old farmer who was found tottering in from the field proved to be of especial service in determining, the mental status of Martin Kallikak Jr. In introducing herself, the field worker had spoken of her interest in Revolutionary times and of having come to him because she had been told that he was well informed as to the history of the locality. "Yes," he said, with excusable pride, as he led the way to the kitchen steps descending into the garden, "not much has happened in this place for the last seventy years in which I have not taken an active part. Do you see that tree there?" and he pointed to a fine maple that threw its luxuriant shade over the path that led to the barn. "The day my wife and I came here sixty years ago, we planted that tree. It was a little sapling then, and see what it has become!" After much more talk she cautiously put the question, "Do you remember an old man, Martin Kallikak, who lived on the mountain edge yonder?" "Do I?" he answered. "Well, I guess! Nobody'd forget him. Simple," he went on; "not quite right here," tapping his head, "but inoffensive and kind. All the family was that. Old Moll, simple as she was, would do anything for a neighbor. She finally died — burned to death in the chimney corner. She had come in drunk and sat down there. Whether she fell over in a fit or her clothes caught fire, nobody knows. She was burned to a crisp when they found her. That was the worst of them, they would drink. Poverty was their best friend in this respect, or they would have been drunk all the time. Old Martin could never stop as long as he had a drop. Many's the time he's rolled off of Billy Parson's porch. Billy always had a barrel of cider handy. He'd just chuckle to see old Martin drink and drink until finally he'd lose his balance and over he'd go! But Horser — he was a case! I saw him once after I'd heard he was going to marry Jemima. I looked him over and said, 'Well, if you aren't a fine-looking specimen to think of marrying anybody!' and he answered, 'I guess you're right — I aren't much, but I guess I'll do fer Jemima.'"

"Such scandals as there were when those girls were young!" he continued. "You see, there was a fast set of young men in B— in those days, lawyers, who didn't care what they did. One of them got paid back, though, for Jemima wanted to put her child on the town, and they made her tell who was its father. Then he had to give something for its support, and she gave it this man's full name. I saw him one day soon afterward and he was boiling with rage. All the comfort I gave him was to

Great-grandson of "Daddy" Kallikak.
This boy is an imbecile of the Mongolian type.

Malinda, Daughter of "Jemima"

FACTS ABOUT THE KALLIKAK FAMILY 89

say, 'I don't see but what you're getting your just deserts, for if anybody wants to play with the pot, they must expect to get blackened!'"

"By the way! Do you know that old Martin had a half brother Frederick — as fine a man as the country owned — who lived about twenty miles from here? You see, Martin's mother was a young girl in Revolutionary times when Martin's father was a soldier. Afterwards he went back home and married a respectable woman."

"Did you ever see the mother of old Martin?" the field worker asked. "No, she was dead before my time, but I have heard the folks talk about her. She lived in the woods not far from here. Dear me!" he went on, "it's been so long since I've thought of these people that many things I forget, but it would all come back to me in time."

Two daughters of Jemima lived in B—. A little study of Chart V, sections A and B, will place them in their relation to the rest of the family and give the chief facts of their lives. Little more need be added. One of them was early put out to service and later married a cobbler to whom she has borne many children. She is not known to have had any illegitimate offspring, but if she escaped, her daughter has made up for her deficiency in this respect. The other sister grew up in the mountain hut with her mother, and was living there when her grandfather died. Her husband and most of her children are defective, but there are two by unknown fathers who are normal. One of these, a girl of considerable ability, supports herself and mother in a decent way and is respected by her townspeople. The mother is tall, lean, angular, much resembling Jemima, except that the latter was even more masculine. Many are the living inhabitants of B— to whom the old woman was a well-known figure, for she often came down into the town bringing berries to sell, her large feet shod with heavy boots, her skirts short, while her sharp, angular features were hidden in the depths of a huge sunbonnet. She thus formed a striking picture that could not easily be forgotten.

A third daughter of Jemima had gone to Brooklyn to live, and the question kept repeating itself, "What will she be like?" and this all the more because of the uncertainty of the parentage on the father's side. Perhaps he was a normal man. Perhaps this will prove to be a normal woman and so break the dead monotony of this line of defectives.

In a back tenement, after passing through a narrow alley, the home of this woman was found. It was about ten o'clock in the morning. After climbing a dark and narrow stairway, one came to a landing from which a view could be had of the interior of the apartment. In one room was a frowsled young woman in tawdry rags, her hair unkempt, her face streaked with black, while on the floor two dirty, half-naked children were rolling. At the sight of a stranger, they all came forward. The field worker made her way as best she could, across heaps of junk that cluttered the room, to a chair by an open window through which a breath of outside air could be obtained. On the bureau by the window a hideous diseased cat was curled in the sunshine. The mother, Jemima's daughter, was not at home, but the woman who had presented herself was her daughter, and these were the grandchildren. The woman's feeble-mindedness made it possible to ask her question after question, such as could not have been put to a normal person. Her answers threw a flood of light upon the general depravity of life under such conditions. When the mother at last arrived, she proved to be of a type somewhat different from anything before encountered in this family. She appeared to be criminalistic, or at least capable of developing along that line. Unfortunately, the visit could not either be prolonged or repeated, so that no satisfactory study was made.

Great-grandchildren of "Old Sal."

Children of Guss Saunders, with their Grandmother

In the city, the individual is lost in the very immensity of the crowd that surrounds him, so that his individual actions, except such as he himself chooses to reveal or can be made to reveal, are lost to the people about him; therefore there was little hope of obtaining much side light on the problem here presented. During the short interview the older woman showed unmistakable signs of wanting to appear respectable in the midst of her depravity, something quite characteristic of the high-grade moron type in the family. She was friendly and distinctly more intelligent than her daughter, but there was little more will power or ability to cope with the problems of life. One of her daughters had disappeared off the face of the earth a few years before — there had been a baby — that was all they knew. She was working at Coney Island. One day she came home and, when she left the next morning, it was the last they ever saw of her. A brother of the girl had also disappeared in much the same way.

The field worker left the tenement with the positive assurance that environment without strict personal supervision made little difference when it was a question of the feebleminded.

Owing to the courtesy of the County Superintendent and the intelligent cooperation of the teachers, it was possible to apply the Binet tests to all the descendants of Martin Kallikak who could be found in the schools. The request for this had been made in a way to give no clew to the particular purpose underlying the search. By selecting from every class one or two bright pupils to take the tests along with the dull ones, all personal element was eliminated. As children everywhere are found to delight in the tests, only those who were not called out were disappointed.

A morning was spent in a schoolhouse situated on the top of a bold, rocky ledge that went by the picturesque name of Hard Scrabble. It was within a quarter of a mile of the ruins of Martin Kallikak's hut, and a number of his descendants were enrolled among its pupils.

One of the grandsons of "Old Sal" lived on a farm near Cedarhill, several miles farther up the ridge. This man, Guss Saunders by name, had been reported to be the father of a large family. Nothing, however, had been learned of him beyond the facts stated, and therefore the inference was that he had turned out better than the rest of his brothers. It had been to determine this matter that the long ride was undertaken.

Arrived at the farm, the question of the mentality of this family was quickly answered. Desolation and ruin became more apparent at every step. The front of the large farmhouse was quite deserted, but following a few tracks the back door was reached. Such an unwonted spectacle as a visitor attracted instant attention. The door opened, revealing a sight to which, alas, the field worker was only too accustomed. She gazed aghast at what appeared to her to be a procession of imbeciles. The tall, emaciated, staggering man at the head braced himself against a tree, while the rest stopped and stood with a fixed, stupid stare. Quickly regaining control, the field worker said pleasantly, "Good afternoon, Mr. Saunders. I hope you don't mind my intruding on you this way, but you see I am looking up the children of the neighborhood, and I was sorry not to find any of yours in the Cedarhill school to-day." He at once thought he had to do with a school inspector, and his answer bears no setting forth in print. It was an incoherent, disjointed, explosive protest against school laws in general and fate in particular. It was mixed up with convulsive sobs, while his bleared, swollen eyes brimmed over with tears. The field worker began to feel real sympathy for the man, although she knew that he was drunk and that drunkards are easily moved to tears. "Oh, I am sorry for you," she said; "your wife then is dead, is she?" "Yes, she's dead!" he answered with a wild gesture, "they took her right out of that room — they said they'd cure her, if I'd let her go. You can see the doctors in B—, they know all about it — they'll tell you what they done — they took her away, and she never come back — Oh!" Stifling his sobs, he went on, "And now they say I am to send my children to school — and what can I do ? Look there!" pointing to a lump of humanity, a girl who, at first glance, had thrown her imbecilic shadow over the whole group, making them all look imbecilic — "do you see that girl? She's always fallin' into fits, and nobody can't do nothin' with her." Breaking in here, the field worker said, "But, Mr. Saunders, you ought not to have the burden and the care of that girl; she could be made so happy and comfortable in a place where they understand such cases. You ought — " The field worker could get no farther. His eyes suddenly assumed a wild, desperate look and he burst out, "No, no! They'll never get her. They tried it once, but they didn't get her. They took my wife away and she never came back — they'll never get her!" A few soothing words to allay the storm she had unconsciously raised, another expression of sympathy, and the field worker drove away, pondering deeply the meaning of what had been seen and heard.

We have come to the point where we no longer leave babies or little children to die uncared for in our streets, but who has yet thought of caring intelligently for the vastly more pathetic child-man or child-woman, who through matured sex powers, which they do not understand, fill our land with its overflowing measure of misery and crime? Such thoughts as these filled the mind of the field worker on the ride home.

Arrived at B—, her first care was to obtain an interview with the doctor who had attended Guss's wife when she died. She found him ready to explain all he could of the family which he had always known and attended. "The mother," he said, "was a kind-hearted, simple-minded soul, who tended as best she could to the needs of her family." The epileptic girl, he explained, had always been a great care, and the doctor himself, aided by several prominent citizens, had taken the trouble to complete all necessary arrangements for having her admitted to the epileptic colony at Skillman. The father, however, could never be made to give his consent. The mother was still quite young when she was carrying her eleventh child. Some accident happened which threatened her with a miscarriage. The doctor was summoned. He saw that it was a serious case and sent for two other physicians in consultation. It was decided that an immediate operation was necessary, if the woman's life was to be saved. They succeeded in persuading Guss to allow her to be removed to the hospital. Their efforts, however, were unavailing; she died under the operation.

On the outskirts of B— lived the owner of the Cedarhill farm worked by Guss Saunders. He proved to be an intelligent man, with an admirably appointed home. He was keenly alive to the needs of the family, about which the field worker came to inquire. "The pity about Guss," he began, "is that he can never let drink alone. Why, do you know, if I paid that man wages, he'd use every cent for rum. I ceased giving him money long ago, for if I had, the town would have had to look after his children. I give him credit at the store, and they supply him with what he needs."

The foregoing glimpses of the defective branch of the Kallikak family must suffice, though the field worker's memory and notebook contain many similar instances.

In turning to describe the other branch of the family, two difficulties confront the writer.

First, the question of identification. The persons already described are either gone and have left nothing behind them by which they can be identified, or, if living, will never recognize themselves in this book.

The opposite is true of the good family. Some of them will recognize themselves, but the public must not discover them. To insure this, the writer must refrain from telling the very facts that would give the story its most interesting touches.

The second difficulty is that a description of the activity of a normal family of respectability and usefulness is never as interesting as the bizarre experiences of the abnormal.

Hence the reader will find in the following sketches only such facts as will show the thoroughly normal and regular family life of the intelligent citizens of a commonwealth.

In a certain village of New Jersey, lying picturesquely on the crest of a hill, is a graveyard where Martin Kallikak Sr. and several of his immediate descendants lie peacefully at rest. He had in his lifetime a great passion for the accumulation of land and left large farms to most of his children. These farms lie in the vicinity of the aforesaid village. Some of them are still in the possession of his descendants, while others have passed into strangers' hands. On the hill above this village is a stucco farmhouse in a fine state of preservation. It belonged to Amos — lineal descendant of one of the colonial governors of New Jersey and to Elizabeth, daughter of Martin Kallikak Sr. The farm is, at present, in the possession of the widow of Elizabeth's grandson, the latter having been a minister in New York City. In renting the farm, the family has always retained a wing of the house, which, although remodeled, still presents much the same appearance as in the days of Amos and Elizabeth. There is the same fireplace, the same high-backed chairs, the clock, desk, and china cupboard. Every summer the family has come back to the old place to enjoy the country air, the luscious grapes and other fruit planted by their ancestor.

On another hill, less than two miles distant, lives a granddaughter of the same Amos and Elizabeth. Her father had been, in his day, one of the wealthiest and most prominent citizens of the community. In an old desk, part of his inheritance from his mother, was found a number of valuable papers belonging to the Kallikak family. One of these is the famous deed of the original purchase made in 17— by Casper Kallikak, signed by the governor of the colony. These papers the daughter guards with great pride. She is a woman of ability and manages her large farm with admirable skill. The splendid old homestead, which has been remodeled and fitted up with all modern conveniences, was built by her mother's ancestor. Although she is deeply interested in all family matters, she has been too much engrossed in business affairs to have given this subject much attention. A daughter of hers, however, who has inherited the taste, has been able to make up for her mother's lack in this respect. The young woman is now married, and her oldest son bears the united name of his two ancestors, the colonial governor and Martin Kallikak.

Miriam, the oldest daughter of Martin Sr., married a man who was a carpenter and a farmer. Although of good family, yet, for some unknown reason, he was not personally acceptable to Martin or his wife. Miriam died when only thirty-six years old, and her husband married again. In his will, Martin makes no mention of his grandchildren by this daughter. They have been respectable farming people, but have never held the same social position as the other members of the family.

Martin's third daughter, Susan, married a man descended from a family conspicuous in the colonial history of New Jersey and which counts among its members one of the founders of Princeton University, while a collateral branch furnished a signer to the Declaration of Independence. One of Susan's sons is still living, having attained the advanced age of ninety-eight. He is a resident of the town that bears his family name and has always been conspicuous as a loyal and upright citizen. To-day, the old man has quite lost his mental power but retains his courteous manner and placid gentlemanly countenance.

In a central region of northern New Jersey, remote from any direct line of travel, lies a town named for one of the families connected with the earliest settlement of the colony. This family rose to distinction in many of its branches, but honors itself chiefly for having produced one of the most brilliant advocates of the cause of Independence of which New Jersey can boast. He was descended on his mother's side from the first president of Princeton University and took his degree there before he was sixteen years of age. From this family, Martin Kallikak's youngest son, Joseph, chose his wife. It is interesting to note that the descendants of this pair have shown a marked tendency toward professional careers. One daughter, however, married a farmer, and most of her descendants have remained fixed to the soil. Another daughter married a prominent merchant, and this line, having been fixed in the city, has produced men chiefly engaged in mercantile pursuits; but the sons, of whom there were five, all studied medicine, and although only one of these became a practicing physician, their children have carried on the family tradition in this line.

On the outskirts of another New Jersey town, in a beautiful old homestead, inherited from his mother, lives a grandson of Frederick Kallikak, oldest son of Martin. He is a courteous, scholarly man of the old school. His home is rendered particularly attractive by the presence of his southern wife and two charming daughters. In his possession are numerous articles belonging to his great-grandfather. This gentleman manifested such an intelligent interest in giving information in regard to his family that it seemed a question of honor to inform him as to the purpose of the investigation, laying bare the facts set forth in this book. He proved to be, perhaps, the one man best qualified in the entire family for entering into an analysis of its characteristics, and this he did freely, in so far as it would serve the ends of the investigation.

Another descendant of Martin Kallikak Sr., a granddaughter of his youngest child, Abbie, had been previously informed regarding the same facts. This lady is a person not only of refinement and culture but is the author of two scholarly genealogical works. She has, for years, been collecting material for a similar study of the Kallikak family. This material she generously submitted to the use of the field worker. In the end she spent an entire day in the completion and revision of the normal chart presented in this book. No praise can be too high for such disinterested self-forgetfulness in the face of an urgent public need. We owe to these two persons most of the information which has made possible the study of the normal side of this family.

Of Martin Kallikak Sr., himself, the record of many characteristic traits has been preserved. As stated in another chapter, his father died when he was a lad of fifteen. The father, in his will, after enumerating certain personal bequests to his wife, recommends the selling of the homestead farm, in order to provide for the education of his children. There is a quaint document still in existence, in which Martin Kallikak, having attained his majority, agrees to pay £250 to each of his three "spinster" sisters, still minors, in return for a quitclaim deed of the homestead farm. This was a considerable burden for a young man to assume, but it seems to have given him the impetus which later made him a rich and prosperous farmer.

He had joined the Revolutionary Army in April, 1776. Two years later he was wounded in a way to disable him for further service, and he then returned to the home farm. During the summer of enforced idleness he wooed and won the heart of a young woman of good Quaker family. Her shrewd old father, however, refused to give his consent. To his objections, based on the ground that Martin did not own enough of this world's goods, the young man is recorded as saying, "Never mind. I will own more land than ever thou did, before I die," which promise he made true. That the paternal objection was overruled is proven by the registry of marriages, which gives the date of Martin's union with the Quakeress as January, 1779.

The old Bible of Casper Kallikak, one of the family heirlooms, is in the possession of a Reverend Mr.—, who is descended from Casper through the line of one of his daughters. This Bible was bought in 1704 and is still in an excellent state of preservation, for, although time-stained, the pages are intact and there still may be seen in legible handwriting the family record penned so long ago. On a flyleaf, is a quaint verse in which old Casper bequeaths the volume to his eldest son, bidding him, "So oft as in it he doth looke" remember how his father had "aye been guided by ye precepts in this booke," and enjoining him to walk in the same safe way.

Chapter V

What is to be Done?

No one interested in the progress of civilization can contemplate the facts presented in the previous chapters without having the question arise, Why isn't something done about this? It will be more to the point if we put the question, Why do we not do something about it? We are thus face to face with the problem in a practical way and we ask ourselves the next question, What can we do? For the low-grade idiot, the loathsome unfortunate that may be seen in our institutions, some have proposed the lethal chamber. But humanity is steadily tending away from the possibility of that method, and there is no probability that it will ever be practiced.

But in view of such conditions as are shown in the defective side of the Kallikak family, we begin to realize that the idiot is not our greatest problem. He is indeed loathsome; he is somewhat difficult to take care of; nevertheless, he lives his life and is done. He does not continue the race with a line of children like himself. Because of his very low-grade condition, he never becomes a parent.

It is the moron type that makes for us our great problem. And when we face the question, "What is to be done with them — with such people as make up a large proportion of the bad side of the Kallikak family?" we realize that we have a huge problem.

The career of Martin Kallikak Sr. is a powerful sermon against sowing wild oats. Martin Kallikak did what unfortunately many a young man like him has done before and since, and which, still more unfortunately, society has too often winked at, as being merely a side step in accordance with a natural instinct, bearing no serious results. It is quite possible that Martin Kallikak himself never gave any serious thought to his act, or if he did, it may have been merely to realize that in his youth he had been indiscreet and had done that for which he was sorry. And being sorry he may have thought it was atoned for, as he never suffered from it any serious consequences.

Even the people of his generation, however much they may have known about the circumstances, could not have begun to realize the evil that had been done. Undoubtedly, it was only looked upon as a sin because it was a violation of the moral law. The real sin of peopling the world with a race of defective degenerates who would probably commit his sin a thousand times over, was doubtless not perceived or realized. It is only after the lapse of six generations that we are able to look back, count up and see the havoc that was wrought by that one thoughtless act.

Now that the facts are known, let the lesson be learned; let the sermons be preached; let it be impressed upon our young men of good family that they dare not step aside for even a moment. Let all possible use be made of these facts, and something will be accomplished.

But even so the real problem will not be solved. Had Martin Kallikak remained in the paths of virtue, there still remained the nameless feeble-minded girl, and there were other people, other young men, perhaps not of as good a family as Martin, perhaps feeble-minded like herself, capable of the same act and without Martin's respectability, so that the race would have come down even worse if possible than it was, because of having a worse father.

Others will look at the chart and say, "The difficulty began with the nameless feeble-minded girl; had she been taken care of, all of this trouble would have been avoided." This is largely true. Although feeble-mindedness came into this family from other sources in two generations at least, yet nevertheless these sources were other feeble-minded persons. When we conclude that had the nameless girl been segregated in an institution, this defective family would not have existed, we of course do not mean that one single act of precaution, in that case, would have solved the problem, but we mean that all such cases, male and female, must be taken care of, before their propagation will cease. The instant we grasp this thought, we realize that we are facing a problem that presents two great difficulties; in the first place the difficulty of knowing who are the feeble-minded people; and, secondly, the difficulty of taking care of them when they are known.

A large proportion of those who are considered feeble-minded in this study are persons who would not be recognized as such by the untrained observer. They are not the imbeciles nor idiots who plainly show in their countenances the extent of their mental defect. They are people whom the community has tolerated and helped to support, at the same time that it has deplored their vices and their inefficiency. They are people who have won the pity rather than the blame of their neighbors, but no one has seemed to suspect the real cause of their delinquencies, which careful psychological tests have now determined to be feeble-mindedness.

The second difficulty is that of caring for this large army of people. At the lowest estimates of the number needing care, we in the United States are at present caring for approximately one tenth of the estimated number of our mental defectives. Yet many of our States think that they are now being overtaxed for the care of these people, so that it is with great difficulty that legislatures can be induced to appropriate money enough to care for those already in institutions. It is impossible to entertain the thought of caring for ten times as many. Some other method must be devised for dealing with the difficulty.

Before considering any other method, the writer would insist that segregation and colonization is not by any means as hopeless a plan as it may seem to those who look only at the immediate increase in the tax rate. If such colonies were provided in sufficient number to take care of all the distinctly feeble-minded cases in the community, they would very largely take the place of our present almshouses and prisons, and they would greatly decrease the number in our insane hospitals. Such colonies would save an annual loss in property and life, due to the action of these irresponsible people, sufficient to nearly, or quite, offset the expense of the new plant. Besides, if these feeble-minded children were early selected and carefully trained, they would become more or less self-supporting in their institutions, so that the expense of their maintenance would be greatly reduced.

In addition to this, the number would be reduced, in a single generation, from 300,000 (the estimated number in the United States) to 100,000, at least, — and probably even lower. (We have found the hereditary factor in 65 per cent of cases; while others place it as high as 80 per cent.)

This is not the place for arguing the question or producing the statistics to substantiate these statements. Suffice it to say that every institution in the land has a certain proportion of inmates who not only earn their own living, but some who could go out into the world and support themselves, were it not for the terrible danger of procreation, — resulting in our having not one person merely, but several to be cared for at the expense of the State. These statements should be carefully considered and investigated before any one takes the stand that segregation in colonies and homes is impossible and unwise for the State.

The other method proposed of solving the problem is to take away from these people the power of procreation. The earlier method proposed was unsexing, asexualization, as it is sometimes called, or the removing, from the male and female, the necessary organs for procreation. The operation in the female is that of ovariectomy and in the male of castration.

There are two great practical difficulties in the way of carrying out this method on any large scale. The first is the strong opposition to this practice on the part of the public generally. It is regarded as mutilation of the human body and as such is opposed vigorously by many people. And while there is no rational basis for this, nevertheless we have, as practical reformers, to recognize the fact that the average man acts not upon reason, but upon sentiment and feeling; and as long as human sentiment and feeling are opposed to this practice, no amount of reasoning will avail. It may be shown over and over again that many a woman has had the operation of ovariectomy performed in order to improve her physical condition, and that it is just as important to improve the moral condition as the physical. Nevertheless, the argument does not convince, and there remains the opposition as stated.

In recent years surgeons have discovered another method which has man advantages. This is also sometimes incorrectly referred to as asexualization. It is more properly spoken of as sterilization, the distinction being that it does not have any effect on the sex qualities of the man or woman, but does artificially take away the power of procreation by rendering the person sterile. The operation itself is almost as simple in males as having a tooth pulled. In females it is not much more serious. The results are generally permanent and sure. Objection is urged that we do not know the consequences of this action upon the physical, mental, and moral nature of the individual. The claim is made that it is good in all of these. But it must be confessed that we are as yet ignorant of actual facts. It has been tried in many cases; no bad results have been reported, while many good results have been claimed.

A more serious objection to this last method comes from a consideration of the social consequences. What will be the effect upon the community in the spread of debauchery and disease through having within it a group of people who are thus free to gratify their instincts without fear of consequences in the form of children? The indications are that here also the evil consequences are more imaginary than real, since the feeble-minded seldom exercise restraint in any case.

Probably the most serious difficulty to be overcome before the practice of sterilization in any form could come into general use would be the determining of what persons were proper subjects to be operated upon.[1]

This difficulty arises from the fact that we are still ignorant of the exact laws of inheritance. Just how mental characteristics are transmitted from parent to child is not yet definitely known. It therefore becomes a serious matter to decide beforehand that such and such a person who has mental defect would certainly transmit the same defect to his offspring and that consequently he ought not to be allowed to have offspring.

---

1 At present eight states have laws authorizing some form of asexualization or sterilization. But in all these cases the practice is carefully restricted to a few inmates of various specified institutions.

The Mendelian Law

In 1866 an Austrian monk by the name of Gregor Mendel discovered and published a law of inheritance in certain plants, which, after lying practically unknown for nearly forty years, was rediscovered in 1900 and since then has been tested with regard to a great many plants and animals.

Mendel found that there were certain peculiarities in plants which he termed "unit characters" that were transmitted from parent to offspring in a definite way. His classical work was on the propagation of the ordinary garden pea, in which case he found that a quality like tallness, as contrasted with dwarfness, was transmitted as follows: —

If tall and dwarf peas were crossed, he found in the first generation nothing but tall peas. But if these peas were allowed to grow and fertilize themselves, in the next generation he got tall and dwarf peas in the ratio of three to one. The dwarf peas in this case bred true, *i.e.* when they were planted by themselves and self-fertilized there was never anything but dwarf peas, no matter how many generations were tested. On the other hand, the tall peas were divisible by experiment into two groups; first, those that always bred true, viz. always tall peas; and secondly, another group that bred tall and dwarf in the same ratio of three to one; and from these the same cycle was repeated. Mendel called the character, which did *not* appear in the first generation (dwarfness), "recessive"; the other (tallness) he called "dominant." The recessive factor is now generally considered to be due to the absence of something which, if present, would give the dominant factor. According to this view, dwarfness is simply the absence of tallness.

This law has been found to hold true for many unit characters in many plants and animals. Since study in human heredity has been taken up, it has been a natural question, Does this same law apply to human beings? It has been found that it does apply in the case of many qualities, like color of hair, albinism, brachydactylism, and other peculiarities. Investigation has of late been extended to mental conditions. Rosanoff has shown pretty clearly that the law applies in the case of insanity, while Davenport and Weeks have shown evidence that it applies in cases of epilepsy.

Our own studies lead us to believe that it also applies in the case of feeble-mindedness, but this will be taken up in a later work to which we have already referred. We do not know that feeble-mindedness is a "unit character." Indeed, there are many reasons for thinking that it cannot be. But assuming for the sake of simplifying our illustration that it is a "unit character," then we have something like the following conditions.

If two feeble-minded people marry, then we have the same unit character in both, and all of the offspring will be feeble-minded; and if these offspring select feeble-minded mates, then the same thing will continue. But what will happen if a feeble-minded person takes a normal mate? If feeble-mindedness is recessive (due to the absence of something that would make for normality), we would expect in the first generation from such a union all normal children, and if these children marry persons like themselves, *i.e.* the offspring of one normal and one defective parent, then the offspring would be normal and defective in the ratio of three to one. Of the normal children, one third would breed true and we would have a normal line of descent.

Without following the illustration further, we see already that it is questionable whether we ought to say that the original feeble-minded individual should have been sterilized because he was feeble-minded. We see that in the first generation all of his children were normal and in the next generation one fourth of them were normal and bred true. We should not forget, however, that one fourth of his grandchildren would be feeble-minded and that two other fourths had the power of begetting feeble-minded children. We must not forget, either, that these are averages, and that for the full carrying out of these figures there must be a large enough number of offspring to give the law of averages room to have full play. In other words, any marriage which, according to the Mendelian principle, would give normals and defectives in the ratio of three to one might result in only one child. That child might happen to be one of the feeble-minded ones, and so there is propagated nothing but the feeble-minded type. It is equally true that it might be the normal child, with a consequent normal line of descendants; or still again, it might be one of the intermediate ones that are capable of reproducing again the ratio of three normal to one defective, so that the chance is only one in four of such offspring starting a normal line.

Let us now turn to the facts as we have them in the Kallikak family. The only offspring from Martin Kallikak Sr. and the nameless feeble-minded girl was a son who proved to be feeble-minded. He married a normal woman and had five feeble-minded children and two normal ones. This is in accordance with Mendelian expectation; that is to say, there should have been part normal and part defective, half and half, if there had been children enough to give the law of averages a chance to assert itself. The question, then, comes right there. Should Martin Jr. have been sterilized? We would thus have saved five feeble-minded individuals and their horrible progeny, but we would also have deprived society of two normal individuals; and, as the results show, these two normals married normal people and became the first of a series of generations of normal people.

Taking this family as a whole, we have the following figures: —

There were 41 matings where both parents were feeble-minded. They had 222 feeble-minded children, with two others that were considered normal. These two are apparent exceptions to the law that two feeble-minded parents do not have anything but feeble-minded children. We may account for these two exceptions in one of several ways. Either there is a mistake in calling them normal, or a mistake in calling the parents feeble-minded; or else there was illegitimacy somewhere and these two children did not have the same father as the others of the family. Or we may turn to the Mendelian law and we discover that according to that law there might be in rare instances such a combination of circumstances that a normal child might be born from two parents that function as feeble-minded. For practical purposes it is, of course, pretty clear that it is safe to assume that two feeble-minded parents will never have anything but feeble-minded children.

Again, we find that there were eight cases where the father was feeble-minded and the mother normal, and there were ten normal children and ten defective.

There were twelve cases where the father was normal and the mother feeble-minded, with seven feeble-minded children and ten normal. Both of these are in accordance with Mendelian expectations.

We further find that in the cases where one parent was feeble-minded and the other undetermined, the children were nearly all feeble-minded, from which we might infer that the probabilities are great that the unknown parent was also feeble-minded.

We shall not go further into this matter in the present paper, but leave the detailed study of this family from the Mendelian standpoint for further consideration, when we take up the large amount of data which we have on three hundred other families. Enough is here given to show the possibility that the Mendelian law applies to human heredity. If it does, then the necessity follows of our understanding the exact mental condition of the ancestors of any person upon whom we may propose to practice sterilization.

From all of this the one caution follows. At best, sterilization is not likely to be a final solution of this problem. We may, and indeed I believe must, use it as a help, as something that will contribute toward the solution, until we can get segregation thoroughly established. But in using it, we must realize that the first necessity is the careful study of the whole subject, to the end that we may know more both about the laws of inheritance and the ultimate effect of the operation.

Conclusion and Resume

The Kallikak family presents a natural experiment in heredity. A young man of good family becomes through two different women the ancestor of two lines of descendants, — the one characterized by thoroughly good, respectable, normal citizenship, with almost no exceptions; the other being equally characterized by mental defect in every generation. This defect was transmitted through the father in the first generation. In later generations, more defect was brought in from other families through marriage. In the last generation it was transmitted through the mother, so that we have here all combinations of transmission, which again proves the truly hereditary character of the defect.

We find on the good side of the family prominent people in all walks of life and nearly all of the 496 descendants owners of land or proprietors. On the bad side we find paupers, criminals, prostitutes, drunkards, and examples of all forms of social pest with which modern society is burdened.

From this we conclude that feeble-mindedness is largely responsible for these social sores.

Feeble-mindedness is hereditary and transmitted as surely as any other character. We cannot successfully cope with these conditions until we recognize feeble-mindedness and its hereditary nature, recognize it early, and take care of it.

In considering the question of care, segregation through colonization seems in the present state of our knowledge to be the ideal and perfectly satisfactory method. Sterilization may be accepted as a makeshift, as a help to solve this problem because the conditions have become so intolerable. But this must at present be regarded only as a makeshift and temporary, for before it can be extensively practiced, a great deal must be learned about the effects of the operation and about the laws of human inheritance.

Index

Abigail 42–43
Albert 38
Alcoholism 34, 41
  children 40
  Guss Saunders, a victim 95
  in the bad family 75
  in the two branches compared 75
  of the good side 43–44
Almshouse 42
Almshouses reduced if feeble-minded were cared for 105
Asexualization 106

Barrah, Eunice 41
Beede 43
Bible of Caspar Kallikak 100
Binet tests in the public schools 79
  used with the Kallikak family 92
B—, the town mentioned 84

Children of Althea Haight 37–38
Colonies for the feeble-minded 105
Colonization, not hopeless 105
Cordelia 40
Cousins marry 40–41
Crime, tendency to, different in different families 72
Criminals 34
  made, not born 66–67
Criminology and feeble-mindedness 66–67, 70–71

Deborah, admitted to the Training School 17, 74
  as she is to-day 24
  her ability in numbers 27–28
  her cousin at the Training School 35
  her half brother 42, 72
  her half brothers and sisters 42
  her half sister 41
  her Institution records 17–21
  her mother, Martha, further history 73–74
Declaration of Independence, signed by relatives of this family 43
Deed from the governor of the colony to the Kallikak family 97
Degenerates 43
Delerium tremens 40
Detention home of the Juvenile Court, number of feeble-minded children found 69
Died in infancy 34
Digdale, Richard L., work of 65

Edwards Family 70–71
Edwards, Jonathan 65
Elmira Reformatory, number of feeble-minded 69
Elopement 41
Environment 71
  and criminology 70
  determines criminality 68
  effect of, shown 37

INDEX

same for both branches 64
Epileptics 34
  "Old Moll" 37
Euthenist, claims 65–66

Feeble-mindedness, how determined 30–31
  difficulty in caring for the 105
  difficulty in recognizing 104
  is hereditary 113
Feeble-minded, number in the entire group 34
  number in public institutions 68
  number in United States being cared for 105
  reduction in the number through segregation 105
  the dupes of others 68
Field workers, their training and methods 86
Frederick 33

Gaston 43
Good family, the 43
  character of descendants 43–44
  defective children brought up in 71–72
Governor of New Jersey, colonial, relation to Kallikak family 97
Gregory 40
Guss 40, 80–81
Gypsy camp 81

Haight, Althea 34–38
Haight, Eva 40
Hardscrabble 93
Harriet 40
Heredity in Jukes family 66
Home for the feeble-minded, Deborah's sister placed in 41–42
Horser 35
  his marriage to Jemima 87
Horse thief 43

Illegitimate:
  children of Martha 41
  number in bad family 33

Illegitimate: child 41–42
Ill fame, kept house of 34, 76
Incendiarism 41
Incest 42
Insane hospitals, number of feeble-minded in 68
  reduced if feeble-minded were cared for 105

James, son of Martin, Jr 35
Jemima 35–37
  marries Horser 87
Jones, Amy 37
Joseph 40–41
  three sons of 79, 81
Jukes family 71
Justin 38
Justin Kallikak, daughter of 72
Juvinile Courts, feeble-minded children found 69

Kallikak, "Daddy" 34–35
Kallikak family, further facts about 78
  bad matings in 111
  stories of the good branch of the 95–99
Kallikak, Justin 41
Kallikak, Martin, Jr 33, 71
  his family compared with the Jukes-Edwards 65, 66
  should have been sterilized? 110
Kallikak, Martin, Sr 33, 43
  a sermon 103
  his sin 103
  joins the militia 33
  wife of 43
Kallikak, Millard 34, 37
  second wife of 41
Killed in accident 41
Kite, Elizabeth S 79

Lavinia 40
Lombroso 70

Margaret 42
Martha, mother of Deborah 41
  character of her children 73–74

INDEX

Massashusettes Reformatory, number of feeble-minded in 69
Matings in the Kallikak family 111
Mendelian expectation 38
Mendelian Law, the 107
Mendelism, applies to human inheritance 108–109
Mental capacity, necessity of determining 70–71
Minister who married Guss 82
Miscarriage 42
Mongolian type 35
Morons 67, 72
Murder, Guss accused 81
Mute 40

Nameless feeble-minded girl 43
  relation to the problem 103
Nathan 34–35
Normal people, in the good branch of the family 43–44
Normal woman in bad family, daughter of Sylvia 37

"Old Horror" 34, 84
Old Max 65–66
"Old Moll" 37, 84
  described 87
  her death 87
"Old Sal" 35, 84

Paula 40
Pauperism and feeble-mindedness 70–71
Placing out 41
Prince 40
Prisons reduced if feeble-minded were cared for 105
Prominent man, sister of, married Millard Kallikak 41
Prostitutes 34
  number of feeble-minded 69–70
Prostitution and feeble-mindedness 68
Public institutions and feeble-mindedness 68

Quakeress, married Martin Kallikak 100

Refinement, an element of, seen in Deborah's mother 73
Resident, an old, of B— 85

Sanders 40
Saunders, Guss, grandson of "Old Sal" visited 93–94
School work for defectives 67
Segregation and colonization not hopeless 105
Sexually immoral, number in bad family 34
  children 40
  on the good side 43
Sheep, flock of, stolen 34
Slums, largely caused by defectives 78
Sterilization 106
  as a solution of the problem 112
Stillbirth 42
Stupidity, compared with criminalistic tendency 73
Sylvia 37
Syphilitic 41
  woman 40

Temperament
  relation to feeble-mindedness and criminology 68
Temperament, differences of, in the Kallikak family 72–73
Thomas 40
Training School at Vineland 35
  Deborah brought to 74
Traits of the family, reappearance of 64

Undetermined, definition 34

Vasectomy 106

Warren 40
Winship, Dr. 65, 70

Zabeth, Rhoda 34, 71